Additional praise for *Unearthing Paradise*:

"*Unearthing Paradise* is a treasure trove of courage and heart by the blessed rabble who inhabit and love the valley it was no stretch to name Paradise. This holy portal into Yellowstone, like its wildlife, trout, birds and people, is threatened but unbroken. May Americans, sundered though we are, unite in the name of our great park and its river and drive the threat out." –**David James Duncan**, author of *The Brothers K* and *My Story as Told by Water*

"Montana has given enough, *enough*, by way of mining. Gold glitters, gold buys, but gold is otherwise useless. Landscape is far more precious—especially Yellowstone landscape. These fine writers remind us how and why." –**David Quammen**, author of *Yellowstone: A Journey through America's Wild Heart*

"A book that had to be written and must be read." –**Walter Kirn**, author of *Blood Will Out*

"*Unearthing Paradise* brings together a cast of distinguished voices lending their words in defense of one of the most remarkable landscapes in the nation. Paradise Valley is a dynamic, ecologically diverse, magnificent and, above all, fragile resource. This anthology will exist as an important bastion of resistance in the face of increasing destructive threats." –**Callan Wink**, author of *Dog Run Moon*

"The most important book you'll buy this year, or maybe any other, *Unearthing Paradise*, is not only a call to action, it's a beauty in its own right. In this day, when so much is threatened by so many, I hope that beauty can, for once, override a bit of the greed. Get it, pass it around, spread the word, let *Unearthing Paradise* be an awakening, not a swan song." –**Pete Fromm**, author of *If Not for This*

Unearthing Paradise

Montana Writers in Defense
of Greater Yellowstone

Unearthing Paradise

Montana Writers in Defense of Greater Yellowstone

edited by

Marc Beaudin • Seabring Davis • Max Hjortsberg

foreword by
Terry Tempest Williams

2016
Elk River Books
Livingston, Montana

FIRST EDITION

Published by Elk River Books, LLP
PO Box 2212
Livingston, MT 59047
ElkRiverBooks.com
press@elkriverbooks.com

Cover art: "Three Bears" by Jim Barrett
Cover design: Megan Eubank, Eubank Creative, Inc.

Visit **UnearthingParadise.org** for more information.

*For all the defenders of the wild,
and to the individuals who have united with
tireless support behind the
Yellowstone Gateway Mines Campaign*

§

In memoriam: Jim Harrison

Thanks to our Sponsors:

James & Lee Ann Arthur
Joseph Bednarik
William B. Bonvillian
The Carter Family
Frank Carter III
Chico Hot Springs Resort
Martha Crewe
Sabrina Crewe
Tom & Connie Dotzenrod
Dan Gerber
Barbara J. Green
Donna Greenberg
Marian Hjortsberg
Bob Hughes
Margot Kidder
William W. Lynch III
Mountain Home Vacation Rentals
Tom & Bonnie Murphy
Robin Ogata
Sharon Parmet
Doug & Andrea Peacock
Tracy Raich
Jeff Reed
Janet Richardson, Karri & Joshua McGough
Marcia Rider
Wendy Riley
Dirk Schenck
Coby Schultz
Jeremy Schultz
Suzanne Sowinska
Dan Sullivan & Elisabeth Revell
Sweetwater Travel Co.
John Taliaferro
Barbara Theroux
Guy de la Valdene

Acknowledgments:

The editors would like to thank the following for their assistance with this project: Bill Campbell, David James Duncan, Pete Fromm, Allen Jones, Erica Lighthiser, The Montana Book Festival, Park County Environmental Council, David Quammen, Michelle Uberuaga, Callan Wink and all the generous supporters of our Kickstarter campaign.

Contents:

Our Fidelity to Place

foreword by Terry Tempest Williams

IT IS HARD TO IMAGINE A GOLD MINE within view from the north entrance of Yellowstone National Park, but given the state of the world at this moment in time, it is possible. Whatever legislation may be in place from the Obama administration could be undone by the zealotry of the incoming administration committed to placing our nation's public lands in the hands of private interests. Never have our lands, our water and the health of our communities in the American West been more at risk, and in the case of Montana, pressure continues to build around more mining for gold, copper and coal. The Greater Yellowstone Ecosystem is vulnerable.

Unearthing Paradise: Montana Writers in Defense of Greater Yellowstone is an antidote to despair. The words of Doug Peacock to Amanda Fortini to Todd Wilkinson to the next generation of Montana writers like Frank Carter, make this anthology a tour de force, hard-edged words crafted out of a love of place protected. Action to conserve these lands has always been the prayer of conservationists. Direct action will become the new liturgy in the Interior West for those of us who refuse to stand by and watch these sacred lands defiled by fossil fuel, mineral exploitation and greed in the era of climate change.

Annick Smith, a long-time resident of Montana writes, "Land lasts longer than blood or love." Know that alongside being writers, the individuals within *Unearthing Paradise* possess a fierce fidelity to this home ground within the watershed of the Yellowstone River, just a few raven wing beats away from America's first national park. We will fight for them in whatever means we have as citizens who recognize our public lands not only as our natural heritage and identity as Westerners, but home to grizzly bears, bison, elk, wolves, cutthroat trout and ruby-crowned kinglets relentlessly singing within lodgepole pines. To protect the soul of this nation, we must protect wild nature, not only for all people, for all time, but for all species, as well. May you read these words carefully, joyfully, and join us in this ongoing Declaration of the Open Space of Democracy.

Introduction
by Max Hjortsberg

AN UNAMBIGUOUS DOOM hit me like a rock through a
window when I first learned that Lucky Minerals, a mul-
tinational mining interest, had just staked claims across
2,500 acres of public land up Emigrant Gulch, followed
soon thereafter by Crevice Mining Group eyeing a similar operation on the northern border of Yellowstone National Park.

I had just returned from Nevada having spent two
weeks in the Cortez Range working on an environmental impact statement for the proposed expansion of the
Cortez Hills gold mine. As part of my introductory safety training I toured the entire operation. I stood on the
overlook of the enormous hole in the ground watching
haul trucks the size of my house slowly crawl toward the
surface with 350-ton payloads destined for the mill to
be crushed and leached with cyanide, so that maybe 15
ounces of gold might be extracted—about a handful.

In other words, I knew exactly what kind of avari-
cious, teeth clacking, tail dragging beast was coming for
us because I had just been deep down in its belly. Here

was the leviathan in my backyard, and yes that matters, don't let the cynics tell you otherwise. We can and must fight for issues that challenge our nation and affect our world, but at the heart of every environmental fight is someone's home, a place worth fighting for, your locale and, more often than not, on our public lands. Whether it's gold, oil or coal, what all of this boils down to is the need for the paradigm to change. In the face of climate change in the 21st century we cannot continue to fall back on business as usual, and that's what makes this and every local, backyard fight a global endeavor.

Gold is nothing more than a commodity and we have plenty of it. The great immutable metal is infinitely recyclable and should be reused and not hidden away in some vault in the Swiss Alps. We don't need to tear into the Greater Yellowstone to get our hands on more gold. Because Paradise Valley and Yellowstone National Park can rightfully be seen as the world's backyard, and not just my own, certainly helps in the PR department, but doesn't mean that your backyard, or anywhere else for that matter is more suitable for such a sacrifice.

As a poet my instinct was to reach for a pen. I wasn't alone. Marc Beaudin and Seabring Davis joined me as co-editors and authors in this venture, fearlessly believing as I do in the power of the written word. We wanted a chorus giving voice to the mountains and rivers. That is how *Unearthing Paradise: Montana Writers in Defense of the Greater Yellowstone* was conceived—a living document assembled to illustrate the astounding beauty and immeasurable wealth of the Yellowstone River and the surrounding landscape and its occupants, both wild and domestic. We reached out to the amazingly diverse community of writers who reside in, or have called the northern Yellowstone region home, and offer the utmost gratitude to the many authors who contributed and to everyone who has supported us along the way.

The scope of the fight has evolved since the first public meetings in 2015. On November 21, 2016, at the urging of the local community and elected officials, the U.S. Forest Service announced a mineral withdrawal on public lands, initiating a two-year segregation, or pause, on mineral exploration and mining activity on approximately 30,000 acres located around the two mining districts in Park County. The segregation allows for a thorough environmental assessment and public input to support administrative withdrawal, which would prohibit new mining on our public lands for up to 20 years. Only an act of congress can protect these areas from mining for the long term.

The mission of *Unearthing Paradise* is to advocate for, and support, effective protections from industrial-scale mining in the gateway to Yellowstone. The withdrawal process will only be successful if there is resounding support from Emigrant to D.C. This written testimony demonstrates that many diverse voices stand united in protecting the ecosystem and our home, and we urge all our elected officials to support this efort, if they haven't already.

We will donate a portion of the proceeds generated from book sales to Park County Environmental Council (PCEC), one of the local grassroots organizations at the forefront of the fight. Ultimately we hope *Unearthing Paradise* will be an inspiration to not only our community, but to others out there campaigning to protect their home, safeguard their water, defend their dignity, and who are fighting for their voices to be heard.

And your voice? Join us in this fight, write a letter, make a call, talk to your neighbor and let your elected officials know you support the withdrawal process and oppose industrial scale mining in the Greater Yellowstone. Also consider supporting the organizations leading the fight. To that end, you can find additional information at the back of this book.

Now dig into the gold *we've unearthed.*

Guarding the Gates of Paradise
essay by Edwin Dobb

MASTERS OF FIRE. That's how shamans were regarded in prehistoric times. But so were smiths, the largely forgotten but similarly ordained individuals who, employing heat in a novel way, converted rock into metal and metal into objects both useful and decorative. According to the Yakut, a once-nomadic people who have lived for thousands of years in the region now known as Siberia, "Smiths and shamans come from the same nest." Both have been initiated into the occult arts. Both travel through the spirit world. Both possess magical powers. Behold and beware: from raw stone comes a bowl, a mask, a blade. Incredible as it may seem today, there was a time when such transformations were considered as miraculous as turning water into wine.

Jump to the 21st century, well into the age of disenchantment. What was once extraordinary has become routine. The new masters of fire are international mining conglomerates hell-bent on extracting and smelting mineral ores on a scale and at a rate sufficient to satisfy the ever-growing appetites of an urban-industrial civilization that includes billions of people. By means of this audacious new alchemy, we subordinate entire mountains of rock to human intention, converting them into buildings, bridges and railroads, along with all manner of vehicles and machines, appliances and gadgets, including our so-called smart devices, made possible by a newly exploited class of minerals called rare earths. Every year we go to greater extremes, both technologically and geographically, to acquire tin, iron, lead and nickel; copper, silver and molybdenum. *Earth first*, as a provocative pro-extraction bumper sticker says, *we'll mine the other planets later.*

But simply because an activity is commonplace doesn't mean it is wholly or even mostly under our control. Nor does it mean the consequences are always and everywhere desirable. As the smiths knew well, wresting ores from the earth and subjecting them to fire is a risky endeavor, and very likely an affront to the gods. Consider what's at stake. What took nature millions of years to forge we would dare re-forge in a matter of days. Creation, the world as it is, doesn't suit us. We can do better. And we can do it faster.

The proper term for this attitude is hubris. And one of its contemporary signatures is the sacrifice zone, a speculative phrase first used to designate areas that would be permanently devastated following a nuclear attack, but which also is a good match for landscapes where the damage caused by large-scale industry—steel mills, chemical plants, oil refineries, mines—is grave and enduring.

One of America's premier sacrifice zones is located in Butte, an early outpost of the industrial revolution on the American frontier. Despite the extensive cleanup that's taken place in the upper Clark Fork River watershed—at a cost of more than $1 billion so far—a large portion of the physical legacy of mining will never be erased, most of it in Summit Valley, where Butte is located: The Berkeley and East Continental Pits, along with the intervening and surrounding expanses of contaminated waste rock, as well as the Yankee Doodle Tailings Pond, an immense impoundment whose earthen berm holds back decades' worth of toxic slurry produced during the milling process (the first step in separating valuable minerals from the rock that contains them). All of this, as well as the flooded mines, must be monitored and maintained in perpetuity.

But while taking the measure of Butte we should remember that the primary product of mining there was copper, a metal that benefits anyone who relies on electricity or enjoys indoor plumbing, which is to say, all of us. It may surprise some to learn that copper also is essential to many renewable energy technologies, including solar panels, solar water heaters and electric cars. One contemporary wind turbine, for instance, contains between 700 and 8,000 pounds of the metal. That bears repeating: It can take up to four tons to build a single wind turbine. If we don't mine copper we won't be able to harness wind on a scale that would allow us to swear off fossil fuels. Any misgiving we might have about what happened in Butte—and is continuing to happen, since the East Pit is still operating—is also a misgiving about the lifestyle Americans now take for granted. To indict Butte is to indict ourselves.

The same can't be said for the two mines that have been proposed for the southern reaches of Paradise Valley—in Emigrant Gulch and near Crevice Mountain. Here the moral calculus is simpler. Given the proximity of the sites to the Absaroka-Beartooth Wilderness, Yellowstone National Park, and the Yellowstone River, the longest undammed river in the lower 48 states, one could make a compelling case for prohibiting all forms of industrialized mining, including for copper. If shitting where we eat is folly, doing so where we worship is irredeemable lunacy. But the situation is even more absurd

8

than that, because the primary object of the prospective Paradise Valley mines is gold. And there is no justification for locating large gold mines in proximity to such spectacular natural treasures, an irreplaceable legacy all of us hold in common.

The brief against gold is as simple as it is persuasive. About 80% of all gold mined in the world is used for jewelry. To produce enough gold for a single 18-karat wedding band, up to 20 tons of ore and waste rock must be removed from the ground and stored somewhere. The costs associated with the needless trinkets and useless tons are many: permanently ravaged habitat; contamination of groundwater and streams by sulfuric acid, arsenic and an array of harmful metals; and the wholesale degradation of the aesthetic and spiritual features of the land via all of that as well as roads, power lines and the other standard furnishings of industrial development. And as if that were not enough, a final insult: Only a handful of people benefit from the sacrifice. Their magic formula is to achieve short-term private gain by means of long-term public loss and liability. Behold and beware: the perverse alchemy of contemporary capitalism.

In the face of opposition, to be sure, Lucky Minerals has withdrawn its application for an exploration permit on the public lands portion of the Emigrant Gulch project, though the company intends to move forward with exploration on its private claims, pending approval from Montana Department of Environmental Quality (DEQ). And Crevice Mining Group, which insists that its mine will be small, is currently stalled. (In April, 2016—and again in September—the DEQ turned down the company's exploration proposal due to inconsistencies in the scope of the project, requiring Crevice to submit a new application.) But the history of hard rock mining tells us that the time to start holding a mining company accountable is before the state weighs in, including regarding exploration—in other words, when a project is being conceived. And the need for early vigilance is even greater for gold prospects in regions where wildlife and clean water are abundant. Since we agree that under no circumstances should our cathedral be demolished, let's make sure no demolition crew gets anywhere near the building. Exploration makes sense only if everyone agrees that development is acceptable.

After regulatory agencies issue the first round of permits and momentum is established, they often behave more like mining partners than oversight bodies. They are inclined to continue permitting—approving further exploration, the transition to excavation and production, cleanup bonds that invariably prove to be grossly inadequate, expanded excavation—and they are all but powerless if a company goes bankrupt, which small and medium-size outfits tend to do, especially in the face of market fluctuation, and the market for natural resources always fluctuates. Always. Corporations want the same rights people enjoy but only until the day they're presented a bill for damages. Then they suddenly dematerialize. Unlike in Butte, where ARCO-BP, one of the largest, richest and most stable companies in the world, is being forced under federal Superfund law to pay for remediation and reclamation, responsibility for any grave and enduring harm that Lucky Minerals or Crevice Mining Group might do would almost certainly be borne by the citizens of Montana.

Should the prospect of mining in Emigrant Gulch and near Crevice Mountain turn out to be only a temporary scare, the episode nonetheless underscores the ever-growing threat extractive industry poses to public lands, not only within those lands but, as in this case, along their borders, which are rarely congruent with ecosystem boundaries. In the absence of organized and sustained resistance, industrial encroachment will increase throughout the West, whether it be gold mining only a mile outside Yellowstone Park, oil and gas drilling within sight of Teddy Roosevelt's cabin in the North Dakota national park that bears his name or uranium mining near the rim of the Grand Canyon.

Given our chronic restlessness, staggering numbers

and fondness for cities and machines, we probably have no choice but to continue converting certain areas into sacrifice zones, as difficult and painful as that may be. If there is no free lunch, how much will an endless buffet cost? But at the same time we should be creating buffer zones around the places most worth saving. This is not a new idea. But it is one whose urgency is increasing. The only way to properly protect such singular wonders as the Absaroka-Beartooth Wilderness and headwaters of the Yellowstone River is to prohibit industrial and urban development in the regions immediately surrounding them. However benign or well-intentioned mineral exploration might seem, it is the first stage of encroachment, and encroachment is where the battle line should be drawn—where we must stand guard.

[Adapted from "Lost Landscapes," originally published in *Montana Quarterly*, 2016.]

Riches
essay by Richard S. Wheeler

LONG AGO, I BOUGHT A FEW GOLD COINS. They arrived by U.S. mail, registered and insured. I opened the package and soon found myself holding several mysteriously heavy Canadian Maple Leaf coins, gleaming in the morning light. Queen Elizabeth graced one face of the coins. Canada is, technically, a monarchy.

I bought them for the sake of comfort. Gold can be exchanged for vital goods and services in times of social disorder. Gold is a hedge against inflation. Gold was a medium of exchange after the first world war, when it took a million German marks to buy a loaf of life-giving bread. A person with a few gold coins is a person armored against disaster when money is worthless. The coins buy serenity in a world gone crazy.

The Canadian coins were elegant, made from the purest gold that mankind can produce. They are .9999%

fine; there is no finer gold on earth. American Golden Eagles or South African Krugerrands don't match the purity of Canadian gold. I did not buy the gold as an investment. It usually fares poorly as an alternative to ordinary stocks. My coins, which I purchased for about four hundred dollars, are worth twelve hundred now, but were a bad investment compared to shares of most any solid company invested in for that length of time.

Gold is now torn from the earth at great cost. Once it was panned from stream beds, where it had accumulated over eons, and then it was ripped from mineralized rock, sometimes as a mine's primary mineral, but more often as a by-product. Gold was a by-product of the gigantic copper mining operations at Butte, Montana. The mining leaves its cruel mark upon the land. One can see, on the Interstate near Butte, the remains of the Beal Mountain mine, which tore apart a mountain, leaving a vast wasteland of naked rock, cyanide leaching ponds, heaped tailings, decaying buildings and unsightly slopes that torture nature's natural beauty. It would take a fortune to repair the slope and heal the damage done to aquifers and replant the native forests. I suspect the cost of repairing that scar upon a Rocky Mountain wilderness would far exceed the value of the gold extracted from the mine. There are other scars throughout western Montana, where gold miners tore up the mountains and left toxic rubble, unfit

14

for man or beast, behind.

The damage is not just aesthetic. The relentless blasting pierced and ruptured aquifers, producing waters laden with heavy metals, including arsenic. These waters still make their way into springs and rivers, eventually poisoning the land and riverbeds. The Berkeley Pit, in Butte, is a sinkhole of toxic water that kills wildfowl and murders life. It would take a herculean effort to clean that water, or fill that giant hole in the bosom of the mountains. The people of Butte, with federal help, have done much to detoxify the ravished land, but it is only a start. Butte is a colorful and absorbing mining town, but the sinister pit, just east of the city, drains the joy and comfort out of the town.

Of all the dangers wrought by mining of precious metals, damage to our water supply is the worst. Mining unlocks poisons. Mining gradually kills off deer and bear, magpies and elk, snow geese and human beings. The minerals, mostly heavy metals, that ruin a water source find their way into aquifers and rivers. They arrive in our daily bread. They transform lush pastures into naked rock.

I wonder sometimes what were the true costs of the gold in my beautiful Canadian Maple Leaf coins. How many animals did that gold torment and kill? How many noble trees and blooming fields? How many lakes and streams? How much sickness in the bones and hearts of the mortals whose nests are permanently fouled? I do not know. There is no way to count the rabbits choking on their vomit, the marmots curled up and dying in their nests, or the deer with mysterious illnesses.

Animal and vegetable life survive on water; clean, sweet, clear, abundant water. And now water itself is threatened from countless sources. Rivers carry plastic trash to the oceans, where the vile heaps of plastic pile up around estuaries and shorelines. The beaches of Rio, the ocean shores of China, the deltas of the Americas are mired not only in white plastic, but with toxic wastes from inland, which are destroying the ecology of the oceans themselves, and with it, our primary source of oxygen. But little prevents mortals from sending their toxic metals and industrial garbage down our streams and into the oceans, where day by day, they take us closer to ending all higher life on earth, including our children and grandchildren.

My beautiful Canadian Maple Leaf coins cost too much.

Satyrikon
or
The Tale of Sadim the Jester
(a Forgotten Fable)
fiction by William Hjortsberg

EVERYONE KNOWS THE STORY of Old King Midas and
his golden touch. Not many remember Sadim, the king's
jester, who spoke and performed backwards, mimicking
his master's every movement in reverse. Sadim was a satyr, hairy goat legs and all, second cousin to lascivious
Silenus, caprine aide-de-camp to jovial Dionysus, god of
wine and pleasure. One of Midas' farmhands found Silenus sleeping off a drunk in his majesty's vineyard. He
brought the creature to the king. Much amused by the
strange half man, half goat, Midas decided to keep Silenus.

Dionysus was very fond of his favorite satyr. Greatly
displeased when he heard the news, the god traveled in
his chariot to Phrygia where Midas ruled. Crowned with
grapes in place of gold, his broad smile a rebuke to the
tyrant's perpetual sneer, Dionysus asked for the return of

Silenus. Midas wanted to know what the god offered in exchange.

Dionysus chuckled at the king's impudence, calling for a goblet of wine. "Running a kingdom must be an expensive proposition," the god said as he quaffed. "I will give you a goose that lays golden eggs."

Midas thought this over, tugging on his beard. "A goose lays but once a day," he observed. "Perhaps something more substantial. It indeed costs a lot to run a kingdom."

Dionysus asked for a second goblet. Tossing back the wine in a single divine swallow, he said, "I grant you a special power. Henceforth, everything you touch will turn to gold."

Well pleased with the god's proposition, Midas slapped palms to seal the bargain. As part of the deal, Dionysus offered the loan of Sadim, Silenus's satiric little cousin, to serve as the king's jester for a year. Once the god departed with his hung-over right hand satyr, Midas raced from one palace room to the next, touching everything in sight. Sadim ran backward right behind him, replicating every regal movement in reverse. "Eureka!" Midas shouted each time his fingertip struck it rich.

"Akerue!" came the satyr's inverted echo.

All the king's retinue followed, howling with laughter, more amused by Sadim than amazed at the golden touch of their sovereign. Distracted by the merriment, Midas paused in his alchemical transubstantiations long enough to see what was so funny. The moment he looked at Sadim's retrograde antics he laughed so hard he nearly cried. "Ishkabibble!" shouted the king.

"Elbbibakhsi!" the satyr shouted back.

Everybody laughed.

According to differing versions of the legend, greedy old Midas got his comeuppance when he couldn't eat because every morsel of food turned to gold as he put it in his mouth or else that he accidentally turned his young daughter into a lifelike golden statue. Neither was true. Midas solved his eating problem by appointing an official "feeder," a royal flunky whose only task was to fork food into his monarch's mouth with a utensil already converted to gold.

The king actually did turn a little girl from flesh and blood into 24 K but she was the daughter of a palace gardener and no kin to Midas. The humble peasant laborer had a dozen other children at home. Losing one was of little consequence, the king reasoned. He gave his gardener the lifelike statue as a sentimental souvenir. "Melt it down and retire in luxury," Midas said.

Soon, Midas transformed everything within reach into gold. His entire palace was gold. All its furnishings: gold. Every tree in the royal garden, each bird perched on their limbs, all gold. Gold everywhere one looked. Golden goats. Golden pigs. Golden chickens. Golden turds in the outhouse. Midas without any doubt was the wealthiest king throughout the ancient world.

Good as gold was Old King Midas until everything went wrong. Like so many tyrants, his majesty's story ended in outright rebellion. Midas couldn't understand why the citizens of the realm were discontent. His subjects had every benefit a monarch might offer. The king funded numerous civic projects with rocks and clay bricks converted to gold. His kingdom boasted miles of aqueducts bringing clean water from the mountains, free entertainment at opulent theaters, splendid gymnasia and public baths. What could the rabble possibly complain about?

Sadim gave him the answer. Whirling like a dervish in reverse, the satyr chanted: "Dnuora erehwyreve si dlog, nwod edispu dna tuo edisni."

"What's he saying?" Midas demanded.

"Inside out and upside down, gold is everywhere around." His major domo, trained to interpret backwards language, translated the satyr's words.

"Dnuorg eht ni tpecxe erehwyreve."

"Everywhere except in the ground."

King Midas did not understand. Sadim kept on spinning and chanting. "Esruc s'rehtona si tfig s'nam eno."

20

"One man's gift is another's curse," the major domo repeated in forward motion.

"Not funny!" the king protested. "He's supposed to be funny."

Sadim spun faster and faster. "Semoc reven gnihton morf gnihtemos."

The major domo struggled to keep up with the jester's ever accelerating speech. "Something … from nothing …never … comes," he pieced together at last.

Midas was furious. "Ridiculous," he fumed.

The little satyr became a blur, his frantic words emerging as if out of a whirlwind. "Dnuow a sniamer dnuof si dlog erehw. Eloh on si ereht, elohw si htrae eht nehw."

The major domo had trouble understanding the hurricane of backward words. Sadim repeated them over and over and over. At last, the functionary pieced together what he said.

"When the earth is whole there is no hole. Where gold is found remains a wound," he told the angry king.

"Riddles?" Midas stomped his foot. "I don't want riddles. Let them at least be funny. What use is a jester who doesn't amuse?"

The major domo no longer listened. He thought about gold pronounced backwards. Dlog. Such an ugly word.

Sadim spun like mad, echoing his riddle again and again in an insane frenzy. The major domo, having nothing new to translate, took a moment to consider what the little satyr was actually saying. The riddle struck a chord. "Your majesty," he said. "I believe the jester refers to a petition yesterday from a delegation of peasants."

"And what of it?" Midas demanded.

"They complained that the countryside has been ravaged, fertile valleys destroyed, entire forests uprooted by a disastrous calamity."

"Can this be true?" King Midas looked dumbfounded.

"Your most esteemed personage must see for himself."

King Midas set out with his royal retinue and a cohort of the palace guard to investigate the peasant's complaints first hand. What he observed was disheartening. Slag heaps and tailing piles where orchards once blossomed. Great raw gouges in the earth in place of lakes and streams. Mountains leveled into rubble. The king could not comprehend the enormity of this disaster. Had evil dragons run amok in his kingdom?

The regal procession came at last to a site of utter devastation. Gray barren wasteland surrounded a single dead tree under which a group of peasants worked melting a golden calf sent to them by Midas. "What seems to be the problem here?" the king inquired.

"You! You're the bloody problem," the angry rabble shouted. "Where do you think your filthy gold comes from?"

The peasant mob rushed forward brandishing cudgels and pitchforks. Recognizing many relatives among them, the royal guard stepped aside. No one wanted to lay hands on the king, fearing instant transformation into gold. Instead, a burly farmer lassoed Midas around his legs and the crowd dragged the king to the barren tree, tossing the other end of the now golden rope over a bare branch.

His royal majesty was hauled up and lowered headfirst into the bubbling cauldron. A gleaming statue of Midas looking extremely displeased emerged from the molten gold like a candied apple. It remained standing for many years at the center of the ruined countryside as a monument to his greed. And what of little Sadim? The satyr scampered back to the Grove of Dionysus where he happily guzzled fine red wine out of a wooden goblet for the rest of his days.

MORAL: All that glitters is not dlog.

Cutthroats
essay by Bryce Andrews

MY ONE, TRUE LAKE is shaped like a deer in its daybed, and it hangs in a cleft of high, hard mountains like a tear at the corner of an eye. The water is clear as cut quartz crystal. It becomes a mirror when the wind quits, and the peaks are forever leaning in to see their faces. When rages take them, the mountains slough stones the size of pickup trucks and refrigerators. Water closes over these boulders, or nearly so, and the lake heaves up a fraction of an inch. The rocks sleep, disturbed only by nosing trout.

When last I wet a line there, I shared the place with strangers. Suffice it to say that they were vacationing, circumstance jumbled us together, and the substance of their professional lives was the ruination at great profit of mountains similar to the ones rising carnassial around my lake. We spoke about it, and of open-pit mining one of them said: "If we didn't, somebody else would."

They ate lunch in yellow autumn sunshine and six inches of melting snow, and afterward one man crossed to the lake's far shore. He stood on a stone, casting clumsily while ripples from his fly mixed with the rise-forms of the lake's abundant, naïve westslope cuts. After scourging the water at length, he caught a slim ten-incher and lifted it by the leader. It made a very pretty picture with the peaks behind him and clouds sailing through clear, blue sky in the shapes of cabbages and anvils. Holding the flashing creature toward his companions, he shouted: "Is this a big one?"

His friends chewed their sandwiches.

"What about it?" he asked again. "Should I keep it?"

No answer came, and after a quarter of an hour his fellows gathered their things. Seeing the shadows lengthening, they struck for the comforts of a lodge. The angler walked last. Passing, he threw the fish into the snow at my feet.

"For your dinner," he said, and was gone.

Not yet dead but far beyond hope, the fish gulped weakly and regarded me with one dark eye. It was thin as a hatchet handle, half-frozen and weightless in my grip. Having no good way to cook it, I set it in the lake.

§

In the morning, I caught and released one cutthroat after another, feeling each fish's electric, jitterbugging strength stir the line and my heart. How could he? I wondered. Why would he take a trout that, fighting on the line, stood in for every fish to ever beat the current—every Coho coming home and every marlin tail-walking over the wide Pacific—and pitch it up the bank to die without a reason?

Dipping my hand into the ice-cold, so-very-clear water to slip the hook, I scrabbled at a corner of the mystery, thinking that most of us are alive inside and relatively whole, while a few luckless others are broken where it counts. A person had to be broken, I supposed, to lift a fish and see just his own strength and mastery finning the sky.

When a whole, healthy, living human catches a fish, he cannot fail to be moved by its foreign, submarine strength and direction. As his little leviathan sprints weightless over stones, he knows that the line between angler and quarry, whether made of monofilament or metaphysics, is old, mysterious and worthy. And by the time that fish gulps air, he knows beyond a shadow of a doubt whether it is right to keep the catch for dinner or send it splashing home.

[Previously published in *Big Sky Journal*, 2016.]

Five Haiku

poetry by Martha Adkins

Eagle is up early
After a snow; black wings
Over the river.

Nothing for you today rabbit,
Except stray oats,
And the whole haystack.

Carefully, quietly
Two magpies are tending
Their bundle of sticks.

Hot spring waters come
Carrying messages from
The belly of earth.

Elk crossing rivers
Old people getting up—
Transitions are risky.

Minefields in Paradise
essay by Myers Reece

INEVITABLY, SOMEBODY WILL SHOUT something about job growth, and a few listeners will nod their heads: Let's go home, boys, the economy is fixed. But in searching for solutions to the increasingly complicated riddles of global capitalism, if mining in Paradise Valley is the answer, I'm not sure I ever understood the question.

More likely, my reasoning is clouded by blue skies and clear water. It's hard to see the dollar signs when I'm staring at native cutthroats rising to my fly, a sight that is no less exhilarating now than it was two decades ago when I first experienced it as a boy violently swinging a hand-me-down fly rod at the fragile waters of the Yellowstone River.

I was born and raised in Livingston. Given my parents' stable of artist and writer friends, it was a lot like growing up in a zoo, only more literate and stinkier. Some of these animals became mentors, and they had the audacity to value silly trivialities like good books and fine cuisine and untarnished mountains—you know, things like happiness. My parents harbored similarly outrageous notions, and I developed an early inkling that life had more to offer than money. It was a terrible training ground for Wall Street, but it's worked out for my writing career.

When I think of Livingston, the institutions that first come to mind are streams and forests, followed distantly by those built by man. Undoubtedly, I learned plenty in school, but my memory drifts far more easily to the lessons absorbed outside those walls. River rocks were the brick-and-mortar foundation of my youth, and they still keep me stable. I have a new baby, and I want to be able to walk along those same wet stones with my kid, listen to the same whoosh of water, and watch the same cutthroats dart to the surface, without wading through arsenic or hearing the distant boom of industry carving gaping holes in the views that framed my childhood.

The Crevice Mountain mine proposed near Jardine, within sight of the northern entrance to Yellowstone National Park, and the Lucky Minerals operation closer to Chico Hot Springs both seek gold in the spirit of

Montana's gold rush in the 1860s and 1870s, though with far more destructive tools and markets. Sure, I get caught up in the whimsy of nostalgia just like the next person, but I enjoy reading about the gold rush in the same way that I like a good book about the Civil War: discovering our history helps us know who we are and how we got here, even if it's ugly.

But our past also provides clues to where we're going and how we should, and shouldn't, get there. Too many examples—Berkeley Pit, Libby's asbestos Superfund site, and Milltown Dam come to mind—offer working templates for the lasting consequences of industry without foresight. History books tell us about the people and decisions that brought forth the environmental damage; it's our responsibility to learn enough from them to both repair the damage and prevent it in the future. We shouldn't take that duty lightly.

I'll admit that I'm not an expert on aesthetics or fashion. Typically, if I dress myself without my wife's help she'll run me down before I get to the door, having identified an egregious violation of the sacred color-coordination commandments. But I do know that Butte's Berkeley Pit is neither pretty nor fashionable in an age of growing environmental consciousness, which is to say that a substantially larger open-pit mine at the doorstep to Yellowstone National Park will be unwelcomed by anybody who is not profiting off the landscape disfigurement. That includes the 4 million people who visit Yellowstone each year. Nor will the warm waters of Chico Hot Springs have the same appeal if you're worried about them poisoning you.

Come to think of it, when I peer into those dark trout eyes as it considers my fly, I'm actually looking at the dollar signs. That's where the real money is, the kind that lasts generations, the kind that's just as fun for our children as for us. People pay a lot to glimpse these treasures. Some build homes and careers here. Others come for the memories. And they'll keep coming, while the rest of us will stay, unless heavy machinery bulldozes the incentive. A gold mine lasts forever, too, but only in its scars and public debt. When the mine taps out, and the river flows dirty, who will come then? I suppose somebody in a future generation will tout environmental cleanup crews as job growth, but is that the way we want to grow?

The Great Surrender
essay by Amanda Fortini

ONE SUNNY, TEMPERATE LATE-APRIL AFTERNOON six years ago, I make the 26-mile drive from Livingston, Montana, the small town of 7,000 where I live, to the nearest city of Bozeman. An hour later, the air is heavy, the sky darkening to the color of dishwater, and all signs point to rain. But my then-boyfriend, now-husband, is returning from a trip that evening, so I ignore the weather, because I want to buy some candles before he arrives. By the time I emerge from the store, snow is beginning to fall. Now I know that when the sky starts glowering like this, it's safest to prepare for the worst, but at the time I anticipate a light dusting. It's spring, after all. Unconcerned, I get into my car.

My route home will take me over the Bozeman Pass, the winding mountain passage on Interstate 90 that joins the Gallatin and Bridger ranges, and sits at the approximate midpoint between Bozeman and Livingston. Driving over "the pass" in the winter is dangerous, and instills a twinge of fear in the hearts of all but the most foolhardy locals. Before we attempt it, we do our research. There's an online webcam that offers real-time pictures of the highest point (elevation 5,702 feet), but to me they always look like the grainy, inscrutable black-and-white images produced by a security camera or a sonogram machine. Usually, someone who has had to drive over the pass—for work, or to fetch a visitor at the airport—posts their snapshot on the Livingston Facebook page, letting other people know of the conditions. News of snow and ice also travels quickly by word-of-mouth through the town's lunch spots, coffee shops, and bars.

I don't yet know about any of this on that afternoon six years ago, because I've just moved to the area, and by the time I reach the pass, I am driving through a blizzard. The snow is coming down with such dizzying density and speed that I'm unable to see more than a few feet in front of me—a complete whiteout. For long stretches at a time, there's no shoulder on I-90, so I can't pull over. Places where I might have stopped are already occupied by cavalcades of semi-trucks whose experienced drivers knew immediately not to press on. In any case, I don't trust that the small Ford hybrid I am driving will keep me safe and frostbite-free while I idle by the side of the highway, with more substantial cars hurtling past, spraying snow from their tires. So I creep along, praying I won't slide into another car, or off the mountainside, trying to suppress the hysteria rising in my chest, promising God that I will no longer be crabby or impatient or late on my deadlines if I could just have some help getting home.

§

When most people learn that you're from Montana, they say something like, "I hear it's gorgeous there," or, "Wow, Montana, beautiful Big Sky Country." They're referring to the landscape, of course, with its immense, unobstructed horizon and blue-tinged mountains that break into rolling sage-covered hills of grayish-green. It is beautiful, almost heartbreakingly so. But that's an idealized portrayal, and such a superficial description of what nature is like here. It assumes that nature is solely pictorial and visual—an image on a postcard, an object you appreciate, an amenity. But in Montana, nature is forceful, astronomical in its magnitude and scale, powerful in its ability to dictate your daily life.

And not only during winter. There are dust storms here that brown out the sky, winds that pinball through valleys at hurricane speeds and golf-ball-sized hail that descends without warning to pockmark the roofs of houses and cars. Four summers ago, my husband and I attended a music festival in Paradise Valley, just south of

Livingston. It was held high in the Absaroka Mountains, so attendees were bussed up. As we listened to the music, the clear late-summer day swiftly turned inclement. I heard the low growl of thunder. Neon bolts of lightning sliced through the sky. The other concertgoers looked up, then around at each other. "Lighting is striking," you could almost hear them thinking, "and we are trapped on a mountain, together." Not ideal. People began to run for the busses, but the concert was still in progress and the vehicles hadn't yet made their way back up the mountain. As a group of us stood there, waiting, the rain falling cold and hard, the sky crackling and flashing, I heard a man's voice loudly drawl: "Mon…fuckin…tana."

Drenched, jittery, jaded and fatalistic from living here, we all knew exactly what he meant.

§

In the early days after I'd moved to Livingston from Los Angeles, I experienced a near-constant state of awe. I couldn't spend enough time outdoors, which was fine, since, unless you want to go see *Kung Fu Panda 3*, that's mainly what there is to do here. The sun-bleached, maize-colored hay fields against the arresting blue sky: I had never seen this combination of colors. It felt visually peaceful, hypnotic. My instinct was to drive around and take it in. Surrounded on all sides by meadows and mountains and sky, I felt the prodigious embrace of the

35

living world. When my boyfriend and I hiked Livingston Peak, or "Mount Baldy," a 9,295-foot crest of the Absaroka Mountains, I gathered wildflowers for the first time, later determining their genus and species names with the help of a book I'd purchased: deep-purple lupine and fiery-red Indian paintbrush. Their colorful, elongated, bell-like shapes reminded me of women in old-fashioned dresses. And the animals! Deer, grouse, magpies, meadowlarks, antelope, foxes, porcupines, eagles, ospreys, bighorn sheep: they enchanted me as though I were a child. Every cow was an event. "Look, a cow!" I would call out from the front seat of the car, during our regular Sunday afternoon drives. "It's … a … cow," said my boyfriend's adolescent daughter, who had grown up here, where bovine life is as familiar as street life in New York.

It did not take long, however, for me to realize that my chief relationship with the natural world would not be as a beholder of it. Living here, nature becomes a part of every decision. You come to understand that dealing with it is not optional, a choice, like going to a park. It's not uncommon to meet up with a grizzly bear on an afternoon hike. Or with a rattlesnake, as I did one summer afternoon while walking through dry grasslands with two friends visiting from New York City. (They looked like they might vomit or wet their pants, and I couldn't blame them.)

But my scariest brush with nature's menacing side involved another cold-weather fiasco. After an evening soak in a sulfurous hot spring, my husband, who regularly launches us on ill-advised adventures, suggested we drive a backcountry route to Great Falls and have dinner there. It was December, so the dark descended quickly: inky, thick, enveloping. We drove for a few minutes until the car stopped suddenly, jolting us forward and back. My husband pressed on the gas. The gears ground unproductively. The tires spun in deep ruts of hard, impacted snow. We were stuck. He tried again. Nothing. We waited for a car to pass, so we could flag down the driver and ask for a push. But an hour later, not a single vehicle had gone by.

I began to panic. I could see a ranch in the distance, but the windows of the main house were dark. Even if we could reach it without freezing—literally—what if no one was home? There was no cell phone reception, so we couldn't call for help. And we didn't have enough gas to sleep in our car. My husband, poker-faced though obviously desperate, found a windshield scraper in the trunk, slid himself underneath the car and painstakingly dug out our tires, while I pedaled the gas whenever he instructed me to. Almost two hours later, the car lurched forward with a loud, pulverizing noise. We returned the way we came. Only then did I notice I was shaking. At the base of the hill, where we stopped for coffee and gas, the attendant listened to our tale and told us, in his affectless Western way: "You guys got lucky. In the winter, we only send search and rescue up there every two days."

§

If this seems like a story about an erstwhile city person who finally becomes aware of nature, that's only partly true. It is, on a deeper level, a story about coming to terms with the reality that great swaths of life are beyond our power to dictate, and that this is terrifying and constraining and liberating and exhilarating, often all at once. It's a story about how there are still some places, like Montana, where nature is so extreme and dramatic that it persists in pushing through the cracks, forcing you to obey its rhythms, instead of the other way around.

Before I moved to Montana, the weather, with a few outlying exceptions—earthquakes, hurricanes, volcanoes —always seemed tame to me, domesticated. We had bent it to our will. Here it remains feral, recalcitrant. It assaults you, demanding that you confront your own fragility. All Montanans are aware that you can set out on a trip, an errand, or a hike, and your course may veer wildly from your original intentions. The road you expected to take is closed suddenly. You are in danger suddenly. You are on your way to have coffee with a friend and you find yourself in a dust- or snowstorm suddenly. Nature here is not benign or comforting, but prone to violence and caprice. It disciplines you. You must contend with it. It is a *force majeure*.

§

These days, I am acquiescent. It is early July, and summer is reaching its climax. After eight months of winter, it is Carnival in Montana. There are nearly 16 hours from sunup to sundown, and the long days induce a kind of mania. The animals are out foraging, eating, mating. The hills and meadows, whose muted, striated colors and varied textures usually call to mind sedimentary rock or a woven Indian blanket, are momentarily lush and electric-green, as though someone decided to plug in the scenery. The natural world is sped up and active, and you, too, find yourself in a pleasant but useless state of euphoria: unable to sleep, uninterested in work, full of grandiose plans—an environmentally induced cocaine high.

By my third summer in Montana, I am accustomed to the sharp upsurge of unfocused energy, the frenzied lassitude, we experience at this time of year. Early on, I would go to a shop or restaurant only to find that the proprietor had closed it to fish, hike or simply absorb a glorious summer day, and I'd feel annoyed, judgmental: *Don't they want to make money?*

Like a lot of people, I'd spent many of my adult summers in a cubicle; I was used to ignoring the seasons. I was also constitutionally impatient, and, having lived for years in big cities, accustomed to satisfying any urge to buy or eat or do something on demand. (A guy I dated in New York used to call me "Demanda.") But now I know that during these short, fertile couple of months, people are tending to their well-being by hoarding their sunshine for the year.

On this July evening, my husband, another couple (she a mixed-media artist who owns a local boutique; he a ranger at Yellowstone National Park), and I have driven 20-some miles out to the Boulder River in the Gallatin National Forest. This spot lies beyond all traces of humanity. Here, you won't encounter street signs, businesses, billboards, or other people. From an overlook at the Natural Bridge Falls, where the river rushes wildly over limestone rock, the four of us share a joint and bask in nature at its most glamorous. We are at the natural world's equivalent of Los Angeles' Chateau Marmont, and we are entertaining ourselves with celebrity watching. In the clear, bright summer evening light we see a bald eagle, a pair of Hungarian partridges, a wolf with haunting, colorless eyes, a chubby porcupine toddling along the gravel road and a black yearling bear ambling on all fours away from a public restroom. I feel a giddiness rise in my chest. My work has languished for days, and, uncharacteristically, I don't care.

Over time, living in Montana has pounded into my consciousness the notion that no matter how we fight it, whether with technology, our wills or sheer denial, we are natural beings subject to forces greater than ourselves. It is strangely therapeutic to accept that nature is a reality you're constantly being forced to yield to, physically and practically. By giving in to its ineluctable pull, you begin to see yourself as part of it, rather than in perennial struggle with it. You loosen your grip. You revise your sense of time. From this surrender comes the pleasurable sense that you're having a deeper experience than one born of your own decisions. You are having a collective experience, a cosmic experience, with all living beings energized and activated, or de-energized and de-activated, seasonally, meteorologically, astrologically.

Sometimes the natural world takes your power, as it does deep in February, when every fiber of your being wants to hibernate. Sometimes it bestows you with power you never imagined you could possess, as it does during the peak of summer, when you don't need much sleep, and you feel like you're riding along with all of the motions of the universe. Sometimes it terrifies you with its awesome brutality, as when you are driving alone on a mountain pass and encounter a blustery springtime blizzard. Just as there are receptors in the brain for drugs—like THC and psilocybin—I like to think we have receptors for nature as well. We may believe we are run by our thoughts and anxieties, our urges and our choices, but come to a place like Montana and you will be reminded that the moon is running you. The sun is running you. The light or lack of light is running you. You are the full moon. You are the rushing river. You are the animal, moving and being moved.

[Excerpted from an essay that originally appeared in *Good Magazine*, 2015.]

Town
poetry by Michael Earl Craig

Town was holding its annual pageant
down by the river.
Floats and kettle corn.
Clowns, horns, stuff like that.
The first float came into view.
Not really a float.
It was a men's plaid sport coat
just floating down the river toward us
face down with arms akimbo.
It rippled noiselessly past us.
For a few minutes nothing happened.
Then came the Shriners, swimming in
white underwear. Hats above water.
Yelping. Struggling. A couple of them
disappeared beneath the surface.
Then it was quiet. Nothing happened.
Probably five minutes passed.
Then a homemade-looking raft
with a slippery-looking hog on it
came into view. The hog was covered
with brown spots. Leeches!
someone shouted. People laughed.
Not everyone. No one was sure.
It's a greased hog on a raft with
maybe leeches someone said.
It's not grease someone said.
It's maybe sunscreen someone said.
Those leeches aren't biting said a man

holding a stiff slice of pizza.
The river sparkled. Big trucks moved
ant-like up a mountain in the distance,
belching blue puffs. If those are leeches
said a young mother holding her baby
I say they're friendly leeches.
Leeches ain't always evil said another.
Then the baby who was maybe six months old said
"opportunistic leeches."
He blinked, working his fingers.
"That's our greased hog."
His voice was deep and calm.
"Covered with opportunistic leeches."

Death Horse of a Different Color
essay by Todd Wilkinson

PEGASUS: The mythological pearl-white stallion conceived by the gods. A steed graced with wings enabling it to soar through the sky. Even now, it hovers above as a mystical, inspiring eternal constellation in the cosmos.

When I think of Pegasus, a different Montana-made appellation comes to mind, a name attached to an ill-fated hard rock mining company with a Canadian parent, a now-defunct firm that flew off into the sunset. Like the stars in the heavens, this Pegasus, too, leaves behind a legacy. All we have to do is connect the dots.

After filing for bankruptcy two decades ago, this Pegasus shirked its reclamation obligations on the slopes of the Little Rocky Mountains in north-central Montana.

I remember how, as a young reporter, I waded through one of seven polluted streams descending from the industrialized Zortman and Landusky Mine complex, the waterway's floor coated in coarse tailings and laden with heavy metals, rendering the water unfit for human consumption. I think of several sloppy spills of deadly cyanide that occurred nearby and how the ineptitude of state and federal mining regulators, more or less, allowed it to happen for far too long.

I think of how the public got stuck holding the bag for millions of dollars in remediation and a clean-up job that has no end in sight. I think of the day I asked the media flack working for Pegasus if his employer—then seeking an expansion permit to extract ounces of gold from megatons of earth using cyanide as a binding agent—would really deliver on the promises it was making.

"Trust us," he told me. "We'll leave Zortman, Landusky and the Little Rockies in better shape than we found them."

It turned out to be a lie.

How important is clean water? Ask the mothers of young children on the adjacent Fort Belknap Indian Reservation who have worried about their kids ingesting contaminants. Ask residents living around the Little Rockies if mining left the area richer or poorer.

I am not anti-mining. Far from it. I am all about accountability, transparency and decision-making that considers long horizon lines. In economics, there is a concept known as externalities that basically means industries or individuals passing along their costs of doing business to society.

As a journalist who has written about mining issues for several decades, I have encountered many examples of broken commitments, busted communities, environmental wreckage lying in the wake of hard rock mines, and worries about how to heal epic landscape-level scars. Today, I remain dubious about the promises mining companies make.

Nearly every single mining executive says his or her company will be better and smarter than the other companies that came before. Nearly every single one portrays a scenario in which mining will create jobs and prosperity stretching toward evermore. Nearly every single mining executive, who needs to leverage the attractiveness of mining in order to woo speculative investors, tells local communities and the discerning media they care about the big picture.

Across the West, there are thousands upon thousands of river miles sullied by historic mining wastes. Some of those stretches have turned river channels into lifeless blights where no vegetation grows and aquatic insects are scarce and, if there are fish, they'd be unhealthy to eat.

There are abandoned mines small and large on public and private land that have cumulatively required billions of public tax dollars to mitigate environmental messes.

The fact is that we are not building any more Paradise Valleys or Yellowstone National Parks or Smith Rivers or Bristol Bays.

I am not anti-mining, but when I wander behind our cabin in the Tobacco Root Mountains, my hiking cleats get caked in orangey, strange-smelling mounds of gooey "soil" too toxic even for dandelions to grow. I look at Montana's state flag and the motto "*Oro y Plata*"—silver and gold—emblazoned beneath a sublime environment, and I sigh.

In fact, the history of mining in Montana is one of epic abuse of people and terrain, broken promises and politicians who allowed themselves to be bought and paid for by companies that treated our state as a natural resource colony.

Butte—the poster child for what I'm talking about—was once called "the richest hill on earth." The copper that came out of the ground there was coiled into copper wire that helped bring electricity to a huge percentage of homes in America. But how have the externalities been amortized across generations?

Mining boosters always offer a scenario of prosperity on the cum. When communities become dependent on mining jobs, they cannot contemplate other possibilities. Butte sacrificed human lives to the dangerous mining shafts and when the mavens of prosperity claimed that going underground was no longer economical, the city allowed itself to be disemboweled with open pit mining that destroyed neighborhoods. When the copper was played out, what remained?

Butte still is inhabited by hard-working, resilient, tough-as-nails people, but it is a city that was used up and left for dead by the Copper Kings and their successors. The Berkeley Pit is a rising toxic soup that sits, as a strange kind of headwater to the largest linear federal Superfund site in America.

How did the Copper Kings' wealth creation scheme enrich Butte? The enduring legacy of William Clark (who bought himself a seat in the U.S. Senate) and Marcus Daily is the fowled Clark Fork River, once one of the greatest rivers in the West and today struggling to be put back together again, like Humpty Dumpty.

I am not anti-mining, but as I've driven across Nevada and entered some of the modern mining boomtowns—their ephemeral survival shaped by the fickleness of commodity prices—I'm not convinced by the claims that mining wealth floats all boats.

I am not anti-mining, but why did the U.S. public have to spend at least $155 million to stabilize the Summitville Mine in Colorado, to prevent the Superfund Site from turning into a wholesale disaster? Part of the answer resides in the fact that the Canadian company, Galactic Resources Inc., was declared financially insolvent and incapable of fulfilling its clean-up obligations.

I am not anti-mining, but why did the president of the United States have to intervene to help stop another Canadian company from re-opening the New World Mine on the back doorstep of Yellowstone during the 1990s? Why did it take so long for Canadian mining giant Noranda to realize there are some places which, over time, are infinitely more valuable than gold?

While cultural romantics would have you believe otherwise, as they venerate the 19th century era of prospecting, nothing about industrial strength mining in the 21st century is quaint. "Trust us" isn't good enough. There has almost never, in human history, been a major mine constructed that did not result in a corresponding and inevitable devastating bust that did not leave humans, the local economy and the ecology poorer in its wake. Creating jobs is important, but creating resilient communities compatible with nature are what lasts. Like Pegasus ever-present in the night sky, they are what endures.

Waffles

poetry by Greg Keeler

A creature of habit doesn't deposit its lurid
eggs in just any old nest. There are standards.
Right outside our tabernacle, putrid
curlicues of flesh spackle the lanterns
so that they give off an orangish light.
Using wads of bubblegum for bait,
children sometimes catch trout under a bright
neon sign that says WAFFLES. The gate
to our cemetery is festooned
with iron snails as if that might lend
a little ambiance to this open wound
we call a town. The butterflies that tend
to congregate near runoff from our scenic
mines can be surprisingly photogenic.

Discovery of Wonder(land)
essay by John Clayton

THE 1871 HAYDEN EXPEDITION is world-famous for its study of the region that would become Yellowstone National Park. Its results—the photographs of William Henry Jackson, the paintings of Thomas Moran and the maps, scientific monographs and in-person lobbying of Ferdinand Hayden—convinced Congress to set aside the national park in March of 1872. But the expeditioners' Yellowstone experience didn't begin where ours does today, at an invisible line on the south end of Gardiner, Montana. It began farther north, in the heart of Paradise Valley.

In the spring of 1871 Hayden's crew took a train to Ogden, Utah, and loaded wagons for their long summer journey. They followed a well-trodden road to the Montana territorial capital at Virginia City, then over to Fort Ellis (near Bozeman) where they picked up a military escort. They squeezed their wagons up the narrow canyon of Trail Creek, and realized the wagons could go no farther. So they made a base camp at a ranch owned by brothers named Bottler, along the Yellowstone River, 33 miles north of Gardiner. At the Bottler ranch, high peaks surrounded an open valley strewn with volcanic mesas and knobs. The river lazed along beneath cone-like Emigrant Peak, flowing gently from a tiny notch in the mountainous southern horizon toward a similar notch in the northern horizon. This place was known as the end of civilization, the last permanent residence the expedition would encounter.

For the expedition, in other words, the Bottlers' barns and corrals, where every fence served as a rack to dry the hides of freshly-killed deer and elk, represented the entrance gate. Everything beyond here would be special. This was where the vacation would really begin. Today, most tourists experience the valley between the Bottler ranch and Gardiner, Montana, at 70 miles per hour. But Hayden and his crew—like the Washburn/Langford expedition the year before—were already reacting differently to the landscape.

Indeed, for both parties, one of the most notable aspects of "Yellowstone" was the Devil's Slide. The unusual cliff formation five miles north of Gardiner features several vertical rock bands, including one that looks like a bright red streak running in a slight elegant curve from the top to the bottom of the cliff. The previous year, Nathaniel Langford had been amazed at the immensity of its stark geology, a gigantic playground slide. He wrote, "In future years, when the wonders of the Yellowstone are incorporated into the family of fashionable resorts, there will be few of its attractions surpassing in interest this marvelous freak of the elements." Based on Langford's description, Moran had attempted to draw the slide for *Scribner's* magazine; when Moran arrived in person, he delighted at the opportunity to pause and sketch it at leisure.

Today the Devil's Slide highway pullout would make a great field trip for geology classes. You can envision how the sediments were deposited like a layer cake—one layer full of oxidized iron to make it red—and then later heaved up vertically. A geology teacher would get very excited, and talk about how the sedimentary rocks are of different types, note that they eroding at different rates (thus making the slide stand out), and speculate about how this mountainous land must have all once been at sea level. One of the great things about dry Western climates is that geological features such as this one are rarely obscured by vegetation. You can really see geology, just like when you're in the country away from light pollution and can really see the stars.

But to me the most fascinating thing about the Devil's Slide is its name. The suggestion came from someone in Langford's party, and Langford later admitted that it "was unfortunate, as, with more reason perhaps, but with no better taste, we frequently had occasion to appropriate other portions of the person of his Satanic Majesty, or of his dominion, in signification of the varied marvels we met with." In other words, had they realized how many Yellowstone features they would later name after the devil, they might have chosen a different namesake for the slide.

Yet Langford's first reaction was, sadly, a common one for many of the first Anglos to encounter Western glories: *We need to tell everyone that this is hell.* And maybe the connection was literal: imagine you encounter the slide on a hot summer day in an era before sunscreen. To protect your skin you have to wear long pants and sleeves and a big hat, which become soaked with sweat and rarely get washed. You smell ripe, though not as ripe as the person next to you. You encounter a steep, dry rock cliff, lacking any noonday shade or vegetation or a babbling brook, and colored an inexplicably bright red. You flash onto some preacher's overheated descriptions of a doomed hereafter.

However, some observers ascribe to Langford a more sinister motive. After all, he was an emissary from the upper classes, from robber barons whose belching factories had befouled the East. A crowded New York tenement, shrouded in air pollution and lacking in effective garbage disposal, made for a rather hellish existence—but to keep people there, the robber barons would rather transfer nightmarish images to the frontier. They demanded that the West be portrayed as hell at least until it was tamed by laws, railroads, and mercantile structures—which also happened to be instruments through which the robber barons could extend their wealth and power.

For me, that interpretation feels too cynical. I tend to think of the devil preoccupation as just fear of the unknown. The West was dry, mountainous, and rocky—nearly opposite the gentle, well-watered, long-manicured English countryside that had given Americans cultural expectations of landscape. Americans compared their Atlantic coastal towns to the English seaside, Colorado to the Swiss Alps, southern California to the Mediterranean. The famous paintings of the Hudson River Valley school—and even Albert Bierstadt's more outlandish Western versions—showed landscapes that could have been located in Europe, except for the fact that they were not yet developed. In other words, as a culture America was not yet mature enough to see its landscapes through anything but a European filter. And since a massive, red-streaked cliff couldn't be easily compared to anything in

Europe, it was by necessity intimidating and forbidding. Amazing, yes, but strange, and thus potentially terrifying—special in a way that only the devil could create.

In 1871, Hayden, Moran and Jackson helped push society past that fear. Although they didn't change the name of the Devil's Slide, they did temper public perceptions. When Jackson photographed the slide, black-and-white de-emphasized the red and the protrusions became foreshortened. It wasn't quite so foreign, so easy to make up fiery myths about. Hayden had a similar great gift, documentation and matter-of-fact-ness. Here's his description of the slide: "It is formed by alternate beds of sandstone, limestone, and quartzites, elevated to a nearly vertical position by those internal forces which acted in ages past to lift the mountain ranges into their present heights. As we stand at the base and look up the sides of the mountain, we are filled with wonder at the apparent evidences of the convulsions of nature." Compared to Langford's polysyllabic, comma-laden prose, Hayden just describes the rocks. He shows the evidence. He puts names to the features. He remains eminently practical until the final moment when he shows you the emotion he felt: wonder.

That shift from fear to wonder could have been—should be—the primary contribution of the Hayden expedition to American culture. There's great value to a national park, and there are many natural wonders contained within Yellowstone's current boundaries. But with its powerful combination of art, photography and science, the Hayden expedition was addressing a larger area and a deeper emotional power. *We need not be afraid of western landscapes*, their work said, *we need not violently subdue them.* We can see the wonders of the landscape, and feel them reflected in the wonders of our own souls.

The Battered Wife

essay by Russell Rowland

THE MORE I KNOW ABOUT THE HISTORY OF MONTANA, the more it seems as if my home state is the battered wife in an abusive relationship with mining. From the time they met, back when gold was first discovered in Alder Gulch in the 1860s, mining has been whispering sweet nothings into the ear of Montanans, promising shiny baubles and a lavish lifestyle. The promises weren't entirely empty either, so it was an easy sell. There has been evidence that great wealth is available throughout our vast landscape. From the time a few grubby miners pulled a huge payload from the hills surrounding Bannack and Virginia City, mining has given Montana just enough to keep her coming back.

But while one hand placed a tiny jewel into Montana's palm, the other has, time after time, reached deep into her pockets, pulling out wads of cash for housing, health care costs, even food. But more importantly, mining has withheld the biggest chunks for itself, doling out just enough to the men and women who bent their backs and breathed the poison air to sustain them. It always gave them just enough strength to go back underground and just enough money to afford a few shots of whiskey to forget about how they're unable to buy their wives a nice dress, or shoes for the kids.

Hunger is a powerful reason to stay with someone, no matter how badly they treat you, and mining has consistently kept Montana hungry, while quietly telling her that he is taking the best care of her that he can possibly afford. But from the start, this has been a lie. From the time William Clark and Marcus Daly rigged the tax system so that mining operations paid a fraction of the taxes that other industries (or individuals) paid, to the time W. R. Grace told a boldfaced lie about the effects of their vermiculite on its workers, mining has misled Montana, then tiptoed away in the night when it became clear that they were about to get caught. Clark moved to New York and squirreled away his fortune, leaving millions to his children while the people of Butte struggled to contend with a festering pool of waste. Taxpayers are still paying for this Superfund site as well as the one downstream caused by runoff from that mine.

Libby makes up the third side of a triangle of Superfund sites, with the Milltown Dam in Missoula County making the other—three of the biggest in the country—right here in our home state.

But every few years, when the bruises have healed, and the happy memories have elbowed their way into the forefront again, mining shows up at our door again, with a fine linen suit and teeth shining, opening another tiny box, revealing one more gem. And Montana cannot help but be charmed, and even tempted, hearing those lovely promises, and thinking to herself, "Maybe this time it will be different."

Whisper Past

poetry by Max Hjortsberg

Underneath the shade
cast by the great riparian canopy
embracing the Yellowstone River
quietly explode pods of cottonwood seed,
many small clouds adrift,
some tucked in the palms of our hands
others sailing on the relentless winds
chasing the river on its way
into the heart of the Great Plains.

At the mouth of the canyon
rest the dead that journeyed before us,
their voices just whispers of wind
through tufts of dried grass.
Once like children they came together
singing in a choir beneath a makeshift
roof, hands blackened from laboring
in the earth, tattered clothing crudely mended,
rough voices gentled with harmony.
In the mud outside the muleskinner hollers
at his team, his yells echoing over
their song, a hymnal rising up—
Vain are all terrestrial pleasures
mixed with dross the purest gold
seek we, then, for heavenly treasures
treasures never waxing old.
The wagon heavy, pulling away,
no looking back at Yellowstone City.

Radiance, Paradise Valley, Montana

poetry by Shann Ray

I'm often blind but know stars
fire the indiscernible void, and you
are in my arms again.
At the window where the canons roar
the day of jubilee begins.
Arise, shine, for your light has come
and the glory of the Lord
has arisen upon you.

We live, you say, as if in the bedchamber of those freed
from war. Like flowers with the sun come up

from below. Your hand on my chest, your body
over me you tell me love endures. Everything
grows still. The jump and shout, the luminous turn,
the whisper, the winnowing, the infinite burn.

Bashō in Paradise:
The Narrow Road to the North Entrance
essay by Bernard Quetchenbach

1. MARKING THE NORTHERN BOUNDARY of Yellowstone Park, the Roosevelt Arch beckons at the end of a fifty-mile highway following a legendary river, framed by formidable graceful mountains, across a valley that earns its name each time I pass through it. Something similar to the Roosevelt Arch's call, perhaps, spurred the seventeenth-century Japanese poet Bashō "to be on the road again to cross the barrier-gate of Shirakawa in due time" (97). Revered as one of the island nation's greatest literary figures, Bashō knitted together a walking-tour itinerary linking temples, geographic features, even individual trees where predecessors had composed memorable verses; his travels engendered *The Narrow Road to the Deep North*, a masterwork of haibun, a literary genre alternating passages of prose and verse. Though I live in Billings, one hundred miles to the east, my own journey

can be said to properly begin at Livingston, where I turn away from the Interstate, drive through a narrow mountain gateway, and find myself in a place that has the nerve to call itself Paradise.

2. And why shouldn't it? Route 89 tracks the Yellowstone River between the impressive Gallatin wall and the elegant pyramids of the northern Absarokas. The valley encompasses a generous expanse of usually golden grass, home to a scatter of long-established ranchsteads beset by infiltrating McMansions. If it's winter, ground blizzards might sweep the view away, clearing to reveal eagles and ravens feasting on deer that didn't make it across. Paradise for the birds, and at least transmutation for the deer. Paradise of a sort for anyone lucky enough to be soaking in the shadow of the Absarokas at Chico Hot Springs. Bashō, for his part, also liked his hot spring inns, though at least one was plagued by "the noise of thunder and leaking rain and the raids of mosquitoes and fleas" (110). The settlement around Chico is called Pray. Bashō, no doubt, would have made an offering of linked verses. It's not surprising that this evocative valley has inspired and nourished its own literary community, including Thomas McGuane, Jim Harrison, and the enigmatic Japanophile Richard Brautigan. But soaking, writing, and meditation are not all that is sought here. As in the adage about "them thar hills," the Absarokas are where the gold

is, at least according to Lucky Minerals, high-rollers from Canada. One thing's for sure: Whatever is or will be up there, snowmelt or leaching sulfuric acid, will eventually be down here, too. All tracks, under and above ground, lead inevitably to water.

3. The river constricts into (out of, actually, as I'm going against the flow) Yankee Jim Canyon. Jim George was an irascible northeasterner (different accounts locate his birthplace in Vermont or Pennsylvania) who appropriated the gorge, built a tollgate across the right of way, tried unsuccessfully to hold off the railroad with a lawsuit and a shotgun, and left the place his name. The stone fragments of his hostelry may not be as revered as the warrior monuments encountered by Bashō, but his ornery persistence is perhaps as admirable in its way. In Yankee Jim Canyon, bighorn sheep occasionally pose on roadside crags as they probably did in Jim's day. From here on, especially in winter and spring, bighorns, deer, or elk might be sampling the roadside stubble around each bend, as the alarming "Wildlife in Roadway' signs warn. There could even be buffalo.

4. But not these buffalo at Corwin Springs. These are in fact Yellowstone bison, but they're no longer even relatively free-ranging like their more fortunate peers. Instead, they are internees in a kind of twilight zone, bound either for slaughter or perhaps for relocation to tribal or

private herds. There was a time when Corwin Springs could have offered winter habitat for Yellowstone bison. But the potential range was scooped up by the Church Universal and Triumphant, an eccentric religious sect led by Elizabeth Clare Prophet, while the federal government dithered. Montanans have been famously, though by no means universally, reluctant to accept roaming bison in their midst. There are various reasons why wild bison, like wild wolves and grizzlies, make residents nervous. Animals, especially large animals, don't necessarily comply with human desires. But neither do mountains, rivers or the planet as a whole. That's one thing I'm here to remind myself of. Bashō visited a temple "known for the absolute tranquility of its holy compound" (122). The Church Universal and Triumphant fell into recriminations after the death of its prophet. The buffalo are still waiting.

5. Nearing Gardiner, I pass the Devil's Slide, a curving Gallatin gash that, in fact, does suggest a titanic piece of playground equipment, or maybe the petrified remains of a colossal and challenging Olympiad. Bashō, too, noted distinctive rock formations, recounting each famed outcrop's associated legends and stories. Geologically, Devil's Slide is an expression of the Yellowstone country's earth- and mind-bending deep history, with sedimentary and metamorphic beds tilted almost ninety degrees since

their original deposition. Past the Slide, the mountains close in, holding snow flurries or summer thunder. Electric Peak, the roof of the Gallatins, dominates the view to the west. Over there, across the river, it's already Yellowstone Park, the northwest border frilling out as if the park can't bear to part with these chosen mountains.

6. That knot of buildings ahead in the valley bottom is Gardiner, Montana, complete with the obligatory tentacles of outfitters and motels reaching forward to intercept travelers. But it's a generally unprepossessing gateway burg surrounded by Yellowstone wildness. The Roosevelt Arch is already visible on the far side of town. The Absarokas above are scarred by old mines and nearly abandoned communities like Jardine. Such "semi-ghost towns" testify to the tawdry glory of long-gone gold fever dreams. Having lost his way, Bashō encountered "an old gold-mine once celebrated as 'blooming with flowers of gold'" (117). Picturesque and romantic to be sure. But contamination from abandoned mines is certain to outlast whatever ephemeral riches can be gouged out of the shifting earth. Bashō overnighted at Fukushima, 300+ years before an earthquake jarred its nuclear power plant into a virtually permanent state of disaster. Greater Yellowstone's rugged landscape also teeters on brinks: marginal water supply, supervolcano instability and wildlife already lost elsewhere.

7. But not here, not yet. A couple of miles past the Roosevelt Arch, the Rescue Creek trail crosses a thinly grassed flat. During early summer the path is littered with discarded elk antlers. Earlier still, when snow closes the slopes above, the flat gathers deer and elk, sheep and pronghorns, clumps of grazing bison. You can see all or most of these at once from a pulloff along the Gardner River, a Yellowstone tributary. Even with Gardiner (the two spellings reflect a Washburn expedition misunderstanding) still in sight, an older, saner version of reality spreads across this land that, despite official designations and sometimes heavy-handed "management," still harbors a palpable measure of ecological wholeness and integrity. Bashō's natural and cultural mesh embraced "everything under the sky" (143), as his contemporary editor Soryū concluded about the poet's journey and the book he built from it. Today's travelers seek to reorient distracted perspectives to the emergent mystery of the cosmos, grander than, while at the same time equal to, the sum of its parts. That's what I've come for. And I am here.

8. One might argue that the park is enough, that the land outside the boundary isn't part of Yellowstone. If the Park is "FOR THE BENEFIT AND ENJOYMENT OF THE PEOPLE," as the inscription on the stone arch says, then the land outside that protected zone ought to be for

different purposes, like digging metals from the ground or real estate development. And we can't just say that the products we use should come from someone else's dirt. But this is Yellowstone, a secular equivalent to the "most sacred of all shrines" on Mt. Nikkō, under which, according to Bashō, "its benevolent power prevails throughout the land, embracing the entire people, like the bright beams of the sun" (100). Present-day Yankee Jims know that not only their livelihood, but the very nature of their home place, depends on an intact, viable northern rampart of Greater Yellowstone, which is why places like Chico Hot Springs offer, along with meals and lodgings, a petition to prevent large-scale mining from raining down on Paradise. Consider signing as the toll, or the tithe, for entering the sacred zone. The Chico petition and other public advocacy can claim at least a partial victory: Lucky Minerals has recently given up its claims to public lands above Pray (while retaining private holdings). The "semi-ghosts" of Jardine, however, are twitching as plans emerge for a big mine just a few miles from Gardiner.

9. Wrapped as they are in steel and glass, our travels are more mediated, and more destructive, than those of the haibun master, but we compensate with a destination bigger and wilder than the remotest corner of Honshu. Bashō's travels took him past Koromo-ga-seki, where a feudal nobleman's estate once stood "blocking the en-

trance ... and forming a protection against barbarous intruders from the north." The family had fallen on hard times, its glory "passed into oblivion," and Bashō found little left but the landscape's natural features, "only mountains and rivers" (118). We must live in our limited present, but the contrast between the ephemeral blessings of wealth and success and the more substantial, effectively eternal sources of physical and spiritual well-being offered by the Yellowstone River and its guardian ranges serves to focus a traveler's attention on what lasts, what ultimately matters.

10. Everything flows to water; river valleys are home to many of us and passageways for many more. And water flows downhill. At home in Billings, I often wonder as I walk through Two Moon Park how long it's been since the water I see before me plunged over the falls into the Grand Canyon of the Yellowstone, how long since it flowed through Gardiner, Yankee Jim Canyon, Livingston. I imagine the river's regrets on leaving Paradise and its eager longing for the sea. Like an itinerant poet, a river owes meaning to motion. If "days and months are travelers of eternity," it's no surprise that Bashō found himself "filled with a strong desire to wander" (97). On the plains, the wind usually surges eastward with the river. Once in a while, though, it turns, steering the clouds back upstream. Honoring Bashō's acute, universal per-

ception, I am then "tempted by a cloud-moving wind" (97) to set off once more, bound for Paradise Valley and beyond, following the road to the north entrance.

[All quotations from Bashō and Soryū are from *The Narrow Road to the Deep North and other Travel Sketches*, Nobuyuki Yuasa, translator, Hammondsworth, Middlesex, UK: Penguin, 1966.]

Late Spring

poetry by Jim Harrison

BECAUSE OF THE LATE, cold wet spring the fruit of
greenness is suddenly upon us so that in Montana you
can throw yourself down just about anywhere on a
green grassy bed, snooze on the riverbank and wake to
a yellow-rumped warbler flittering close to your head
then sipping a little standing water from a moose track.
Of course pitching yourself downward you first look
for hidden rocks. Nothing in nature is exactly suited
to us. Meanwhile everywhere cows are napping from
overeating, and their frolicsome calves don't remember
anything except this bounty. And tonight the calves will
stare at the full moon glistening off the mountain snow,
both snow and moon white as their mother's milk. This
year the moisture has made the peonies outside my stu-
dio so heavy with their beauty that they droop to the
ground and I think of my early love, Emily Brontë. The
cruelty of our different ages kept us apart. I tie and prop
up the peonies to prolong their lives, just as I would
have nursed Emily so she could see another spring.

[Previously published in *In Search of Small Gods*, 2010.
Used by permission of Copper Canyon Press and the Estate
of Jim Harrison.]

A Good Country
essay by Brant Oswald

WE HUMANS ARE ALL SHAPED by our physical and cultural environment, but those who spend most of their days out-of-doors are shaped even more directly by the landscape where they live and work. I encountered people in my early life—farmers, ranch hands, loggers, commercial fishermen—who reflected the land around them. I saw the rigors of an outdoor life in weathered skin, deep wrinkles and rough hands, but I also saw individuals who belonged in their piece of the world and who took great pride in that sense of place.

I recall feeling a bit of that sense, returning from my first year of college in Oregon's Willamette Valley, where I had marveled at a landscape lush with fir and white oaks, vine maples and alders. But returning to the sagebrush hills and lava outcrops of southern Idaho that had been my boyhood playground still produced a feeling of belonging, a feeling that I had come back home.

Somewhere along the way from that boyhood in Idaho and school in Oregon, fly fishing took over my life. It had meant abandonment of an academic career and a move to San Francisco to teach fly fishing for a living, which I found to be a perfect job in a less than perfect place. In those years I marveled at the hum of energy created when so many human souls were bought together in a small space, and I reveled in the food and music and art that San Francisco offered. But in many ways, I always felt like a tourist on an extended vacation and not an integral part of the urban environment. And good trout fishing was too far away.

In those San Francisco years, I visited Montana at every opportunity, exploring its back roads and small towns, while testing my fishing skills on every trout stream I crossed. I eventually made the move to Livingston 30 years ago, the result of both careful planning and more than a little serendipity. After only a few months in Montana, I recall returning from a road trip to the Midwest to visit relatives, feeling almost giddy as the "Gil's Got It" signs promised I was nearing Livingston. I had found a new home.

A few years later, work afforded me the annual opportunity to sit down with the matriarch of a local ranching family and listen to stories of her early life in Paradise Valley. One year, I told her I had recently run into some of her relatives on a bird hunting trip in the badlands country near Terry. "It's a good country out there," she said. That turn of phrase struck my ear, but it took a number of years before I came to appreciate what she had meant. It wasn't just a place. It wasn't just the natural mix of landscape and weather and water that allowed a rancher to run a few cows. More than that, it was kids and schools and 4-H projects, it was local politics and squabbles between neighbors, it was a succession of new babies and weddings and funerals. It was a community.

It has taken a long time, but I have come to understand and appreciate a bit of the community I live in along the Yellowstone. As an angler and guide, I view my own life here through the lens of fishing. Fly fishing, whether a private passion or a business endeavor, is ultimately dependent on the resource. Anglers need fish, and fish populations need healthy habitat. For those of us connected to the fishing, our very lives revolve around the conditions that contribute to the health of the fishery. Part of that health is dependent on an ample supply of clean water. We worry about the annual snowpack. Will we get enough snow? Will it fall at the right times to provide reasonable flows throughout the summer? Will we get enough snow and spring rain to cause destructive flooding? How long will the runoff season last? Will flows get so low that water temperatures will be too warm for good fishing? We also worry about threats to water quality. Since most of us don't monitor these conditions directly, we wonder whether bug hatches have changed, whether fish numbers are up or down, whether certain stretches of the river or certain tributaries fish as well as we remember from past seasons.

But there is more to fishing than catching fish. Anglers are drawn to rivers and streams for their intrinsic beauty, for the landscapes that surround them, and for the chance to see the wildlife that live along them. And we enjoy the human community that surrounds our rivers, too. Livingston is a popular destination for anglers from all over the world not just for the fish in the Yellowstone, but also for its small town atmosphere, friendly people, great food, artists and art galleries, and the occasional eccentric bar patron.

That community now faces the threat of the development of mining projects in Paradise Valley. This is not just any kind of mining, but extraction based on sulfide ores and its usual legacy of acid mine drainage. Of course, this is a direct threat to water quality and fish. If a tailings impoundment associated with these mines failed, it could take decades for the fishery to recover. But allowing industrial-scale mining to proceed here also represents a shift away from a proven local economy to a "boom and bust" cycle whose effects go far beyond potential water quality problems. Even absent a water quality calamity, it would result in a loss of the area's character, an issue for all of us, but especially for anyone who owns a business tied to outdoor recreation or tourism.

The Yellowstone drainage does not need another threat to its fishery. There are plenty of threats looming on the horizon already. The Yellowstone, as we often tout, is the longest "undammed" river in the country. Undammed perhaps, at least by major dams, but it is not untouched. Its waters are shared by a variety of stakeholders—there are agricultural irrigators and municipal water utilities in addition to the fisherfolk and recreational floaters. Floating traffic has increased to a level unheard of just a few years ago, with traffic jams at the public accesses and boat ramps.

Even more importantly, climate change has begun to show its effects in recent years. We have seen lower peak flows, with those peak flows coming earlier in the season. Low flows in the summer months, coupled with hotter weather, has meant warmer water temperatures, resulting in afternoon "hoot owl" fishing closures in some seasons to protect the fish population from the stress of angling pressure. The upper Yellowstone and its tributaries are the primary sanctuary for native Yellowstone cutthroat trout, but fisheries managers anticipate invasions into critical cutthroat habitat by species like smallmouth bass that have historically been confined to warmer waters.

As I write in the early fall of 2016, these potential threats to the Yellowstone have become real. The stress of this season's low flows and warm water temperatures allowed a parasitic disease known as PKD to infect fish in the river, resulting in major die-off of mountain whitefish. In order to protect the resource, state officials closed the entire drainage to all recreational use for a period in late August. Cooler weather and water temperatures have allowed the river to reopen, but the impact on the local economy was profound. Even this short-term closure meant a huge economic loss, not just to fishing and whitewater guides and fly shops, but also to every other area business connected to outdoor recreation. In a recent report based on past spending data from non-resident visitors, the University of Montana's Institute for Tourism and Recreation estimate the effect on Park County businesses to be as high as half a million dollars. Given a chance, the river will recover from this outbreak of PKD in coming seasons, but the economic impact to our community serves as grim reminder why we need to protect the resource.

This summer's experience took me back to that conversation at the kitchen table about the woman's relatives who ranched around Terry. "That's a good country," she had told me. But what I remembered best, as I looked out her kitchen window at a rich creek bottom, with the cottonwoods along the Yellowstone and the Absarokas in the background, was the clear gaze and slight smile she directed at me. "This is a good country, too," she said.

It is a good country here. Let's fight to keep it that way.

HeartStones

poetry by Marc Beaudin

The long shadows are suddenly gone
retracted by each host
every tree and shrub holding
a dark double beneath its coat

Evening washes through the valley
as the Yellowstone does–
tasting each rock as it passes
hushing with a finger to wet lips

Once called Elk River
by those who came before &
that other river bleeding luminous above
was at one time the Wolf Road

I was known by other names
as were you
just as there will be new names
for all of this someday

But as I bend
in the gathering darkness
to pick up a heart-shaped stone
from river's ragged edge

I feel that some things are the same
in every language in every time
some things are known and unknown
in the same   voiceless   breath

The stone holds sunlight shimmering through willows
clear waters dancing with trout & transcendence
gold not in the land but of the land
music of magpie raven redtail & bluebird

flicker heron nutcracker egret
pelican osprey nighthawk ouzul
chickadee merganser nuthatch owl
kestrel eagle crow & dozens more

Despite the icy wind cutting
at face & hands
I open my coat unbutton my shirt
& hold the stone to my chest

The double heartbeat fills the valley
resonates on the star-strings taut overhead
leaves me breathing – with whatever breath I have –
breathing with the stones of this river

All of This Begins Here
essay by John Holt

BEING PART OF THE RIVER IS EASY. You just settle into
the canoe, push off from the sandy, gravelly shore and
begin paddling downstream, often letting the current
take you where it will over the course of miles and hours
while the sun seems to soar east to west. Cottonwoods
with thick limbs supporting golden and bald eagles that
resemble stoic statuary slide behind. Willows rustle in a
warm breeze. Herons perch motionless on grey downfall,
eccentric extensions of the dead trees, figures patiently
waiting for small trout or sculpin to move into range of
long, pointed beaks.

The quiet slip of the flowing, living current through
a long, wide bend in the river, the enormous trees lining
the grassy cutbanks, thick tangles of exposed roots dipping into the water, is disrupted by the sound of rushing,
breaking water like strong wind working through the

leaves of these watching trees, the broken water perhaps a quarter-mile ahead. Soon the silvery white crests of standing waves are visible and tangles of deadfalls and limbs slammed together during spring runoff line the edges of the main stem of the river. In a few seconds the pace of the current begins to accelerate, slowly at first, now rapidly and the strength of the Yellowstone is palpable, a force that is basic, direct and potentially overpowering. All effort is directed toward gaining a line through this rough cascade of loud splashing, a line that will hopefully track safely to one side of the three- and four-foot high humps of water that look like the hair standing up on the back of a starving mongrel dog. Paddling is fast and hard as the canoe tries to leak toward the center line of broken water. Time stands still while sun-sparkled water, glistening rock and deep green shoreline run past in a blur of motion and sound. Then the river arcs to the left down below and the relative calm of the inside curve is visible. Hard pushes on the side of the rapids, with forceful J-strokes mixed into the action, maintain the course to smoother going. Then, like none of this ever happened, ever existed, the noise and whirling water recede, and sound vanishes from the senses.

That's being part of the river.

Becoming the river is not so hard, either. Those hours smoothly turn into days, weeks. The swirling and mixing determination of current leads inexorably downstream gradually, but sometimes abruptly, dropping through the country with still more splashing, crested waves and liquid sound and ever nearer to sea level. Paddling becomes second nature, repetitive—even Indian strokes and box-stroke pivots used to maintain course and position in the river are executed without thought. Muscles become routinized and mechanically perform their tasks without pain or fatigue.

Geese by the thousands honking with wild, natural insanity, are now almost subconsciously heard and appreciated, the shimmering vibrations of all those wings in the light have become part of the trip, the natural way of all of the motionless time, a part of the Yellowstone as all of this always has been.

The heat of mid-day, the afternoon upstream wind, the muffled grate of the canoe as it slips across a gravel bar covered with a few inches of water, the whisper of willow and Russian olive leaves, the sound of a small fire crackling in the evening, the buzz of nighthawks feeding on insects and the yelps and howls of coyotes talking with the stars in the cooling air—all of this registers as elements of the river's life on a subliminal stage that has taken over and dominated a clear, basic awareness.

Now the river asserts benign control and draws me into its flow, just moving in and within the water's rhythms. I forget the enclosed, electronic life back home in Livingston. Everything is transformed to the elemental, second nature, happening without effort, without a need to learn or understand. The Yellowstone steadily flows down to the Missouri, then Mississippi and finally the Gulf of Mexico, always as gravity's companion—this movement is the essence of all rivers. The repetitive nature of the day-to-day routine out here is hypnotic, rapidly washing away anxiety and, finally, useless ego.

An unaccustomed serenity and well-being pervades as the canoe tracks its own way with slight help from me.

Everything is now the river and its fertile, riparian corridor with all of the creatures who depend on this water to live moving in synchronicity.

[Excerpted from *Yellowstone Drift: Floating the Past in Real Time*. CounterPunch/AK Press, 2009.]

Liber Mundi

South Fork Deep Creek, Absaroka Range, MT
poetry by Ken McCullough

the moon
   at the lingual edge
Mars the closest
   in 60,000 years
snow, wind, a bull moose
   the waterfall
braiding blue and green
   moss over moss
a numb pool
   Hephaestus
what were you thinking?
   Savonarola
right or wrong?
   This red berry
or not?

Smoke from the Greycliff fire
   sits on Elephant Head
out our window, the creek diverted
   to irrigation ditch
Angus bull drooling and pawing
   Hell Gate, Meat Rack
the map of it
   stitched in my cells
the chill of redemption
   love then and now

[Previously published in *Broken Gates*. Red Dragonfly Press, 2012.]

To the Source:
Sawyer's Paddleabout on the
Yellowstone River
essay by Alan S. Kesselheim

WHEN SAWYER WAS BORN, late one March night in our
bedroom, with the help of a midwife, he was not ready.
His face was red, his fists clenched. If newborns are capable of body language, his screamed, *NOT YET!* For the
first three days of life, he wouldn't open his eyes.

He wasn't an easy infant, either. To call him colicky
might be stretching it, but he needed a lot of soothing; a
lot of walking and comforting. He was one of those babies
that required a two-person team to change a diaper. One
to pin him down, the other to wrestle through his wind-
milling legs and get the damn thing on.

He seemed to have an unaccountable level of frustration pent up. I don't know how else to describe it. He'd
periodically fall prey to alarming bouts of inconsolabili-
ty. Not tantrums, really. More like he was in the grasp of
some sort of anguish and had no way to cope, and that we

had no way to address.

By the same token, he has possessed, from birth, an uncommon awareness of the larger world. Even as a baby, people would look at him and say, "That kid looks wise." Every year, his teachers comment on his perceptiveness. Out of those troubled early times, he has evolved into a sensitive, humorous, likeable young man whose frustration streak only appears in occasional bouts with his older brother.

Here, on this August day, he is thirteen, with the lean build and stamina of a cross-country runner. He is leading the family up the trail to Marston Pass, deep in the Washakie Wilderness of northern Wyoming. The trail switchbacks uphill, leaving trees behind. I'm bringing up the rear. Marypat, the three kids, and the dog, Beans, string out ahead. Alpine valleys, green as velvet, glimmer far below.

It is mid-morning on Day 3 of our family hike. We have already toiled up more than twenty miles of trail, gaining better than 4,000 feet in elevation.

For the second summer running, we are returning to one of the kid's "birth rivers," the flows we paddled when we were pregnant with them. Last year it was Eli's turn, on the Kazan in the barrenland heart of northern Canada. This summer it is Sawyer. The river is the Yellowstone.

At the crest of trail, where the weathered sign confirms the pass at 10,300 feet, the Absaroka Mountains surround us. The Tetons float in the distance. Verdant tundra rolls in every direction. We drop our packs there, but the option of hanging out never comes up. Marypat organizes lunch food, Sawyer grabs water bottles, I pull out a daypack.

The headwaters of the Yellowstone River are close by, within a couple of miles, over a ridge and around a corner, somewhere in the airy, bear-thick wilderness near 11,000 feet. Within minutes we are hiking again, unencumbered by packs.

Beans ranges in front. The trail becomes less and less distinct, then it fades away altogether. We fan out, stay high, contour along the skirts of the valley. Sawyer strides along with his characteristic, intrepid energy, fueled as much by desire as metabolism.

This hike is a pilgrimage. River headwaters are like that—inaccessible by definition, indistinct, elusive, mysterious. There is something undeniably primordial about the source of a drainage, and it exerts an irresistible magnetism.

I think of all the rivers—the Amazon, the Nile, the Congo, the Mississippi, the Yukon. And of the many expeditions mounted over the centuries, the fortunes squandered, the people who died trying, the national pride at stake. Our quest is not on the same scale, but it is no less momentous in the fabric of family history.

During the summer of 1992, Marypat and I paddled the entire Yellowstone with Sawyer's older brother, Eli, in the bow. Eli was eight months old, just thinking about walking, doing some serious teething, and going through diapers at an impressive clip.

Sawyer was along for the ride too, as a fetal bud. He was feeling that jostling current under our red canoe, getting vicarious doses of adrenaline and whatever else pulsed its way through Marypat.

Our hike is Part II of his coming-of-age quest. The repeat descent of the Yellowstone was Part I, played out a month earlier. All of it addresses Sawyer's transition to adulthood.

Besides being the river Sawyer experienced from the womb, the Yellowstone is our neighborhood flow, a river we know more intimately than any one I can think of. Yet, before planning our hike, I couldn't have pinned down its precise beginning within twenty miles. This hike is both an homage to the river, and a metaphor for Sawyer's passage in life.

The Yellowstone is coy to the end. It isn't until we round a final slope that the snowfield nestled above the thin, clear trickle comes into view. Ruby strides to the river's edge. The rest of us follow. It is narrow enough to step across. Downstream the silver thread bends through the tundra grasses, away down the valley.

We spontaneously drop to our bellies, side by side, and sink our faces into the icy, newborn river. We all drink deep, the way we used to drink from mountain streams. The liquid burns going down, sits cold in our bellies, seeps across our cell walls, becomes us.

Our hands are still callused from paddling this river. Our faces and arms are tanned from weeks under the sun, crossing Montana in 25-mile daily chunks. In all likelihood, we still have grains of river sand in our clothes and shoes, even in the roots of our hair. The river we drink from, ten paces from the melting snow that creates it, is embedded in our memories, stamped on our synapses, rooted deep in our imaginations. Like the water we drink, it has become us.

In late June, when we put onto the Yellowstone at the border of Yellowstone National Park, just upstream from the bridge in Gardiner, Montana, the mountains were still cloaked under deep snows. The river was running high, thick with sediment, roaring along, pure and untamed.

At that point the river has already come a hundred miles, more or less, from that snowclad alpine bowl beneath Younts Peak. It has wound its way through the meadows of the Thorofare, pooled in Yellowstone Lake, pounded through the Grand Canyon and Black Canyon inside the park.

We launch with a send-off delegation in a bevy of inflatable craft—a couple of rafts, several inflatable canoes, some kayaks. It wasn't hard to recruit friends. The first day on the Yellowstone is the best whitewater on the entire river, starting with the Gardiner Town Stretch, full of wave trains and loud holes, and ending with Yankee Jim Canyon, with three emphatic rapids, each with boat-eating potential at this water level.

There is no warm-up. As soon as you put paddle to water the rodeo starts. Sawyer straps into a solo inflatable kayak, snaps on a helmet, and pushes off, aiming for a mid-river set of four-foot waves. He has grown up on rivers, starting in the womb and continuing within months of his birth—the Salmon, the Snake, the Gallatin, the Green, the Rio Grande, the Yukon, the Churchill. He barely crests 100 pounds., but he's comfortable in Class III water and already has a river résumé many adults will never achieve.

I watch him pop over the first waves, a red dot in a sea of silty froth, then I scramble into an inflatable canoe and chase after him. The rest of the air-filled parade follows suit.

Within minutes Eli biffs in a side-curler, but he clambers back aboard and powers for the next hole. Ruby, at 11, is in the stern of a tandem kayak with a friend. I watch her fishtail over a wave crest, disappear in the trough.

The day goes like that. It is sunny and warm. People swim. There are a good many whoops and yells. We stop for a picnic lunch where Ruby finds an arrowhead. Yankee Jim Canyon punctuates the afternoon. At the end, all the kids jump into a deep hole off of a bridge.

There we reorganize. Our friends load up for the drive home. We switch to two open canoes, one folding boat and a hard-shell, along with a solo inflatable kayak. We load up expedition style with three-weeks of food, 5-gallon jugs of drinking water, spray decks, the gear that will sustain and shelter and feed us all the way to North Dakota.

We hug our friends, wave goodbye and drift off to our first gravel bar camp as the sunlight goes orange. It feels suddenly subdued, quiet and auspicious, straddling the threshold of the trip.

I can't verify this, but it's my belief that our family has paddled more days and camped more nights on the Yellowstone River than anyone in history. This is our second self-contained, full descent of the river. We have done scores of trips from two days to two weeks. We've paddled the Yellowstone on uncommonly warm weekends in February, and over four-day weekends in October. We've paddled it at floodstage, at low ebb, in wind and sleet, through forest fires and hail storms.

The strange fact is that hardly anyone camps on this

river. It is rafted and drift-boated and canoed, but almost always on day trips. In hundreds of days on the river I've seen fewer than five camping parties. I have no idea why.

Because the Yellowstone is undammed, it acts the way a river should. It moves gravel bars around, refreshes beaches, plants cottonwood seeds, piles up rafts of driftwood, occasionally floods the banks. And because Montana boasts some of the most user-friendly river-access laws in the country, allowing boaters to recreate and camp anywhere below the high-water mark, the river is very available. Beaches, gravel bars, islands, no end of good campsites, complete with driftwood for fires. The fact that no one does it, and that scores of river campers get enticed off to the slow water, poor camping stretches of the Missouri instead, is a mystery to me. But I'll take it.

It takes us several days, and almost one hundred miles, to achieve River Time. It is a moment I wait for, that ambush by the pulse of current and wheel of sun and play of cloud, the point at which we pull free of the tyranny of clocks. Our expedition rule is that watches get left at home, but it still takes a while to get there.

At the end of the third river day, camped on a gravel bar and feeling the new embrace of clockless rhythm, we hold Sawyer's coming-of-age ceremony.

It is a symbolic ritual. The real thing is made up of thousands of paddle strokes, bends of current, pestering headwinds, repetitive camp chores, swimming wave trains, absorbing the lessons that come day-by-day cruising downstream.

We aren't churchgoers. More accurately, we feel the most in church on trips like this one. On top of Younts Peak, for example, with Montana and Wyoming spilling away at our feet. Or in the grasp of roiling whitewater. Or at dawn, with mist melting into the day and a great blue heron stalking the shallows. This is our version of things holy.

So it is completely appropriate that we circle up under the late-day sun with the river rolling past. Because we have no prescribed ceremony for this, we make it up. Sawyer stands in the center. Each of us takes a compass direction. We hold symbols of the elements: earth, fire, water, air. We speak to Sawyer, pay tribute to the earth, and to the web of mystery we are all caught in. We collapse toward him, embrace his lean, strong body. The moment feels awkward and sacred, both.

When we're done, we walk back toward camp. The kids are ready to swim through some nearby rapids again; this camp's roller-coaster ride. Just then, a shadow goes over. We look up. A mature bald eagle coasts directly overhead, not ten feet up. Its head is cocked, fixing us with a yellow-eyed gaze.

We all stop, watch the big bird sail upriver. "Hmmm.

That was cool," I say. "I guess that was for you, Sawyer."

You can make too much of a thing like that, a blessing that feels like more than coincidence, but then, you could not make enough of it, too.

Day on day the river uncoils. We ride its back to the next camp, through rapids, around diversion dams, past cottonwood bottoms. Our time has the feel of Huck Finn on a homemade raft. Civilization lurks on the fringes. We glimpse the interstate highway. Coal trains rumble past. Our boats ghost past the outskirts of towns. We never once cook on stoves, use a firepan and driftwood instead. The moon waxes toward full. White pelicans fish along the downstream ends of gravel bars, deer bound away into the willows, a rattlesnake swims the river near Miles City.

Civilization may be on the fringes, but river life is another dimension altogether. We hunt for agates and petrified wood destined for the rock tumbler in our garage. It is a point of pride that we return from Yellowstone trips heavier than we left. It's a toss-up whether we swim or paddle more of the river. Every day the kids are in the current as much as in the boats.

The Yellowstone is replete with history—Captain Clark's descent on the return from the Pacific in 1806, the Indian wars, the steamboat era, the fur-trade. Maps are full of evocative place names: Lost Boy Creek, Pompey's Pillar, Valentine Flat, Starved-to-Death and Froze-to-

Death Creeks, Sacrifice Cliffs. Chief Joseph and his band of Nez Perce crossed the Yellowstone downstream of Billings in 1877, and headed north, trying to outrun the cavalry to Canada. John Colter yo-yoed up and down the river, exploring and trapping and surviving attacks. Half the cities along the banks are named for military men or battles from the frontier era—Miles City, Sidney, Forsyth, Custer, Rosebud.

Fishermen watch us float past. Faces look down at us from cars on bridge crossings. Train engineers wave and toot. We set off some fireworks on July 4th. We ask everyone we see whether Lance Armstrong won the Tour de France.

At some point around Day 16 or 17, I sense the sand trickling away in the hour-glass. The days become more precious with that awareness. We drift for long stretches, gravity takes us, lazy but insistent.

On some level we have all forgotten that we own a house back in town, that we have friends there, jobs, soccer camps, things to pick up again. Here, life is the swirl of water, the raucous keening of terns, the loom of thunderhead, sand under bare feet. Who needs more?

Then, abruptly, it is the last morning. I am paddling with Sawyer. He is a kid who tends toward silence, but at times comes up with the most outlandish questions. He wants to know how it is that you can put money in a bank and it will grow. When we dispatch with that, he wonders if a meteor hits the atmosphere and happens to enter through an ozone hole, whether it will burn up. Then he wants to learn the lyrics to an old Peter, Paul and Mary tune I've been singing. It's painful, because this kid can't carry a tune in a bucket.

After that we just paddle. Sawyer has a natural stroke with real power. It's the kind of stroke you get when you've been paddling since you could walk—unconscious, unpretentious, supple and efficient. I drop into his cadence. It is a sweet spot, there. Our paddles strike the water in tandem. The boat sings along so that it feels like flying. The bow wake purls toward the Missouri. I think of Captain Clark in his dugout cottonwood trees.

Too soon, around a bend, there it is. We stop and coast toward this storied confluence. Sawyer stands up, strips off his shirt and shorts. Without a word he slips, naked, over the side. I stand up and do the same. Everyone does. All five of us bob in the river next to our boats. The river accepts us, as it has all the way down. We ride together into the mingling with the Missouri, feel the currents eddy together, a visceral participation in the river union.

A few of the water molecules caressing us, perhaps, began in a drop of melt falling from the snout of a snowfield near 11,000 feet almost 700 miles upstream. A spot where, in a few weeks, we will all lie in a row on our bellies and drink deeply.

Where There Is a River as This
poetry by Dave Caserio

I.

Where there is a river as this
 every particle of crap blood-washed and blood-lined.
Where the dead lung of water and the death bellied carp.
Where the river does not glide of its own sweet will
 but frets and gluts.
Where the brown sick foam of the Illinois cataracts
 under Starve Rock—whirls with the Ohio toward the flank
 of the Mississippi.

Where the Illiniwek would not come down but left their
 bones and their children to the dirt-pine and nests of birds,
 to the black-suet, berry seeded shit of bears. Starve Rock.
Over whose edge my father held me be-hawked and
 un-hooded, to clip the dove or talon the pike,
 tight in plummet, wide-swung in wonder.
My father held me, birded and preying,
Over water that no man gives but takes.

II.

"Blind in blind wilderness,
Flash flood,
Hail, wind, rain,
I thought Clark dead.
Only our luck,
Only our perseverance,

Allowed us to live,
To go on naming:
The Dearborn, the Southfork,
Colt Killed Creek, River Philosophy,
The Dog, the Bull, Teapot and Wisdom.
For we made the Panther into the Pipe-Stove.
For the Bitter-Root became Quick Sand.
Elk Rapids our Linchpin and Half-Breed.
For the Judith, wide and timbered—box elder,
Cottonwood, rose bush and honeysuckle.
For Clark's wife this sweet naming.
But Flathead, we kept …

Though they called it, *Koos-Koos ke*
Or, *clear water running*."

III.

Steady flush of blood and matter, the fevered, pustular
 phlegm: hooves, heart, brains, belly, kidney, liver and
 lungs, tail, tongue, and tripe, oil and fat, hide and hair.
Beef-cows of the five great plains.
Sweet-bread of thymus, weasand and snout.
The un-cadenced moan of the stunned calf's skull,
 gelatinous eye in a skim of grease.
Bubbly Creek:
A meat-spackled slime, slop of testicle and ovary,
 crushed trachea and bone;
Of water once water no more:
 chlorinated, sulfuric, ammonia and lead,
 sweet odor of molasses.

101

IV.

Where Potawatomi, Ottawa, Chippewa, deer and grouse—
River of steep hands and sweet marsh.
Where glacial waters ran, down Wolf Ridge, in Panhandle
Wood where cholera woman wanders bald and virgin.
For it is night on the river dead.
Its liquid ventriloquism of light
Through fog and lowland mist, in the whisper
Of plank and barrel, bobbing in regurgitant debris,
In factory and fractured hull, in rust, in ice.
But no dog tooth. No willow.
The cypress gone.

For a river went out of Eden
For man to dress and keep:
For the Pi son of Havilah is of gold and bdellium,
 onyx the stones on its shore.
For second is Gihon that compasseth Ethiopia.
Eastward, the heart of Hiddekel.
Fourth, Euphrates.

Tell me where
Is there a river as this.

[Previously published in *This Vanishing*. Word-Tech Communications, 2014.]

Houseboating the Yellowstone
fiction by Toby Thompson

MIDWESTERN FLOODING KEPT US IN BROOKLYN longer than expected. We houseboaters are an adventurous lot, angling for Hudson River stripers beneath the skyline while arguing city politics, whistling to sirens on the Belt Parkway or admiring chemical sunsets. But summertime on the Gowanus Canal can get sticky. My girl Shady teaches college, so when May arrives we're happy to relocate to cooler waters. Last summer they were Montana's. But June found the Yellowstone unnavigable, and it wasn't until July that we felt it safe to embark.

Our craft is a 22-foot Nyack, its aluminum superstructure mimicking the Airstream trailer's, but sufficiently sturdy, with reinforced hull, to float Montana rivers. We drew stares trailering it across North Dakota, my chocolate lab Darryl slobbering through a porthole, but at Fort Peck we were greeted with knowing smiles.

Houseboating, after all, is a Montana tradition. What was Lewis and Clark's vessel but a primitive Nyack?

We launched south of Livingston at Carter's Bridge. Not having a motor, it was necessary to drift. On certain bends, negotiating haystacks, my flailings resembling Humphrey Bogart's in *The African Queen*. Shady fended off rocks while Darryl braced astern and howled. We anchored near Livingston's fairgrounds.

Of all the summers we've houseboated, I thought, this could be the most delightful. High water had discouraged fishermen, and evenings off the golf course were silent as a South Sea island's. We waded nearby streams for cutthroat, gathered prehistoric rocks, conducted a bird count—19 species during the first week—and pitched sticks for Darryl. At night there were meteor showers and a distant clang from Livingston's freight yards. We cuddled, dozing to the pitch and yaw.

I had checked navigational requirements. There were no ordinances against houseboating on city, county or Fish and Wildlife books. The Sanitation Department had its reservations, but so long as we jettisoned neither sewage nor "gray water" from bath or laundry we were copacetic. The police stayed edgy, but anchoring midstream, we couldn't be chastised for trespassing. There was, however, a catch.

"We get so much petting at boat landings," a cop explained, "we put the whole river off limits." Her eyes narrowed. "Watch yourselves: no hanky-panky."

Her familiarity grated. It reminded me of when Ted Kennedy was photographed *in flagrante coitus* aboard an open Chris Craft, and a Republican colleague quipped, "I see that Senator Kennedy has changed his position on offshore drilling."

Shady was distraught. All year we'd been trying to conceive. Darryl lapped her tears as I assured her that, "Hey, we're adults consorting in private. How might they catch us?"

They didn't, and life proceeded. We moved the Nyack, drifting to Springdale, then trailering it upstream to Carter's. Our favorite anchorage was a tiny bay south of Livingston Country Club. We had a rubber dinghy and were scrupulous about emptying chamber pots. We bathed at Chico, dropped our cleaning at Persnickety, and stashed garbage in county dumpsters. Our living area had bunk beds, a propane stove, a tiny sink and storage niches designed more obsessively than an Idaho sheepherder's.

Shady was on the cell to friends, and by early August they'd arrived: Raphe and Sharon first, Scott and Jenny next, then Howard and Oscar. Three couples, each houseboating, the six of us floating as comfortably as a raft of mergansers. Raphe's boat was a 29-foot Neimitz, with shallow draft and faux-redwood superstructure atop an aluminum hull. Jenny's was an 18-foot Catamaran with a plastic forecastle modeled after Philip Johnson's glass house in New Canaan. And Oscar's was a 30-foot Condor with pink triplex superstructure and umbrellas aft.

Except for cocktail flags snapping and evening laughter, we convoyed unobtrusively behind the golf course. I enjoyed our excursions to town, dining at Pinky's or Gil's, Howard and Oscar—bandannas pasted to their scalps—drinking at the Mint with John Mayer's gang. Livingston authorities grumbled; there was little they could do. A game warden checked my fishing license, a boarding party made life-jacket, passport and narcotics searches, and parents allowed teens to ridicule Howard and Oscar's bikini-thongs.

Shady had won a grant to study urban houseboating, and was on sabbatical. We extended through September, she flying to Seattle and Sausalito for weekends, but returning eagerly to our life. She monitored her temperature and was affectionate. One morning we awoke to snow, the sky cobalt blue, the river incandescent with reflected light, its boulders capped in ivory. That night a miracle happened, we were certain.

Our berth-mates departed. They left their boats until spring, leasing them to carpenters refurbishing the town's grain elevator. Soon after, realtors appeared ... the subtlest on foot, but one—Hugo Frankly—crashing to water's edge in a scarlet Range Rover, its vanity tag reading, SCARF.

Hugo had ideas, concepts. "Houseboating's the last frontier," he proclaimed. "It's low-cost residential housing with B&B status to boot." He gestured at the horizon. "I see a fleet of Sport Sheets from Gardiner to Glendive."

"Sport Sheets," we learned, were sheet-metal double-wides riveted to pontoons. The first craft launched was single-decked and tethered off Ninth Street Island. Its debut was extravagant—champagne, smoked whitefish, braised duck breasts—but police shut down the party when celebrants began urinating starboard. Hugo leased the *Beyonce Bound* to a beautician and her boyfriend for $1,000 a month (sat-TV incl.) and the rush was on. By October, Billion Auto had a line of Nyacks and Shopko was selling nautical doublewides in its lot.

I write freelance, and mid-month left for eight days on assignment. Shady met my return flight. We chatted easily through Bozeman Pass, I patting her stomach and cooing ... but when we hung left at Sacajawea Park I lost it. The change was appalling. Hugo's Sport Sheets dotted the riffles. He'd taken offices in Livingston's Civic Center. His grin was ear to ear. "We run from Whorehouse Bend to KPRK," he bragged. "And that's for starters."

The Sport Sheets' superstructures varied from one to five stories, the largest (*Queen Bee*) as high as the Murray

Hotel. A few were painted chocolate-chip camouflage, after Hugo's "conscientious" objection to the fracas in Iraq, but most were in loud colors: fuchsia, magenta, aquamarine, tangerine-flake, rainbow-swirl, Grateful Dead tie-dye. Hugo paced the riverfront, purring, "This is the dawning of the age of Aquarius—" Within weeks *Queen Bee* had casino gambling and a liquor license. Fancy ladies dinghyed through the gloaming.

We changed berths often. Shady nevertheless was radiant. She eliminated coffee from breakfast, wine from dinner and avoided second-hand smoke. I dozed with my head on her chest, the exhaust fan high to mask harbor chatter. We figured seven months, a June birth. And the wedding? We didn't know. Our plans were Thanksgiving on the Yellowstone, Christmas in Brooklyn.

We spent Halloween aboard the *Fist It*, Hugo's new quadraplex. Shady went as Melania Trump, I as the jokester, Louis CK. It was warm, and re-boarding the Nyack we smooched on deck, stroked each other gently, disrobed. How else to say it? I felt the boat pitch, Shady sigh and we were *Ted-flagrante*, Darryl whimpering from the forecastle. Then we were bathed in spotlight; Shady screamed as a bullhorn croaked, "Hold it!" I fell against her.

She screamed again—this time in pain. She clutched her stomach. A bright trickle stained the deck.

We went before the magistrate on a public fornication charge, were fined and released. The city had its case. It came down hard on the houseboaters, nailing them by spotlight or filming them through night scopes. Gradually the Sport Sheeters departed, jumping leases. Hugo was irate. "Why risk cheap housing for a little Roche Jaune nooky?" Soon he was bankrupt.

We were distraught. Shady spent a night at Livingston Memorial, I in the guest chair by her bed. Then we hauled the Nyack home.

Hearts have a way of mending. Sometimes, watching the lights of Red Hook, Darryl panting beside me and Shady fixing supper, I contemplate our adventure. I miss the big semis' hum on I-90, the stars blinking over Mount Baldy. The Hudson is not our Yellowstone, Gowanus not Livingston. But we're free to cuddle here, to dream.

We wish all sailors well.

[An earlier version of this story appeared in *Firestarter*, 1996.]

Cottonwood

poetry by Frank Carter

Snow sticks to
Your wooden bristles
Dry whiskers grey and brittle
Like a wizard's beard
With the forest
Barren of leaves
The ground a blinding white
On a late November's eve
By the Yellowstone River
The dog and me

The twigs hang down in bunches
Sweeping my hat
Walking under the woods
I disturb the collected cold and
It falls like smoke
Down my back

A deep shiver on hot skin
Exhalation
A trout stirs in dark water
That's when I remember
What I'd forgotten
To make a fire
The perfect kindling

I reach into the long beard
Break and bunch, break and bunch
Into one hand
But don't take too much
I'm reminded
This is where birds sleep
And shelter in storm
Blizzard and squall

My home
Just steps away
Along the icy path
The lights are still on
I see my dear wife
Through the window, illuminated
Swollen belly
Waiting for her fire
To warm together at the hearth
To release the explosive light of the sun
Before sleep

Trout Tears
fiction by Elise Atchison

FRIEDA GRABBED A BEER from behind the bar, popped the top and set it in front of Harold.

"What the hell's this?" Harold said, and he lifted the bottle between his thumb and index finger as if it were a dead rat. "Trout Tears? Really?" He took a swig and grimaced. "Shoulda called it Trout Piss. When am I gonna get a cold Bud around here again?"

"It's all I got, Harold. Chuck and I raided a delivery truck that was parked on the side of Highway 89. They hit a deer, and the front end was bashed up pretty good. We cut the lock on back and took a couple of cases. We got the deer, too. Chuck's going to cook up some venison stroganoff tomorrow night. Dinner in the Chico dining room at seven.

"Yum, roadkill." Harold pushed his cowboy hat back, a hat that had once been white but was now dingy gray from all the days he spent working on his ranch from sunup to sundown. A sweat stained, blood-splattered, cattle-stomped hat that wouldn't fetch a dollar down at the local thrift store. But Harold wouldn't be Harold without that hat. His family had been the largest landowner in the valley before everything went to hell. Now he was squatting in one of the upstairs back rooms of the abandoned Chico Hot Springs Resort, using a kerosene lantern for light and a barrel stove for heat. His face crinkled as he took another sip of his lukewarm beer. "But it's better than nuthin, I guess. Speaking of deer, did you see that one with the teeth growing out of the top of its head? First one I've seen in months and it's a mutant. I don't even know if we should be eating the deer around here since the Accident."

The room went quiet. Mike shifted on his barstool two seats down, his face contorting in the flickering candlelight. No one mentioned the Accident. Ever.

The door opened, and Kim walked in. She took her place on a barstool between Harold and Mike, and everyone started talking again. Mike drained his beer and pushed it forward, his face returning to its usual frozen countenance. Frieda grabbed the empty bottle and set a fresh one in front of him, and she opened one for Kim.

"Trout Tears! Cool!" Kim said, and she smiled at everyone in the sparsely filled room. She was always the

113

cheeriest person in the bar.

But Frieda had seen her standing down by the river day after day. Kim used to spend her days navigating a drift boat full of tourists down the Yellowstone, squinting past the ranchettes and McMansions to the unscarred Absaroka Mountains towering above her. They'd float by kingfishers and trumpeter swans, the shouts of her clients ringing out as they pulled shimmering trout from the churning water. Now Kim stood on the banks of the Yellowstone for hours at a time, staring into the swirl of lifeless water. No swarms of mayflies rising in a thick frenzy over the river. No trout feasting on the squirming bodies of the fallen. No ospreys and eagles diving down to fill their bellies on the bounty of fattened fish. A riot of life now silent, except for the occasional caw of a crow passing overhead on its way to somewhere else. The river was dead, and her fishing guide business died with it. Frieda wondered how Kim managed to stay so annoyingly cheerful in the face of it all.

Mike tried to suppress a hacking cough, and Kim turned toward him. "Hey Mike, how's it going?" He gave a slight nod, more than he ever offered anyone else in the bar, and he went back to peeling the Trout Tears label off his beer.

The two of them used to have fierce arguments about the mine coming into Paradise Valley, but they were all in the same boat now. Everyone was broken, as scarred on the inside as the land was on the outside, but Mike was the most broken of them all. He had been the strongest supporter of the mine, and he had believed, truly believed, in the goodness of gold. When the Accident happened and the company pulled out, he lost his brand new truck, his ATV and boat, even his wife and baby girl who moved out as soon as the paychecks stopped coming in. Mike used to be a loudmouth, but now he never said anything to anyone, he just sat drinking whatever Frieda put in front of him until closing time sent him out into the night. He'd put on his headlamp and hike to his tent on the side of the mountains, a campsite far enough from the mine that he could pretend nothing had happened. Mike had spent a lot of time in the Absarokas before the Accident. He used to go hunting with his buddies, tracking trophy elk through the autumn snow, but nowadays the only thing he spent time tracking down was his next drink. Frieda couldn't bring herself to deny him that one small comfort in his shattered life.

She looked at the shrinking candles. It would be time to close up when they burned out, but they still had a little flame left in them. Frieda opened a beer for herself and took a long, warm gulp.

She knew they weren't supposed to be in the Saloon. Chico closed down after the Accident, and Frieda lost her bartending job. Everyone who had money left the area, and even those who didn't have money had to leave once their homes were foreclosed. Only a handful of stragglers remained, a ragtag band of stubborn misfits who refused to give up on this place.

"It's like when my wife got cancer," Harold whispered a few nights ago. "I didn't run away just because things got tough. I stuck it out. That's the only honorable way to live."

"Yep," Frieda had said, but in truth she didn't see anything honorable about their situation. Every day, every hour, every second she had to face the fact that Chico was a pale ghost of the vibrant gathering place she had once loved. The historic buildings were falling apart in the harsh Montana weather, and the pool had filled in with windblown debris. Kids vandalized the place early on, throwing rocks through the windows and spray painting "Gold Diggers Go Home!" on the side of the Main Lodge. But of course the mining company did go home, right after the Accident. They closed their doors and went bankrupt, leaving the taxpayers to pick up the tab.

It was right after Harold lost his ranch that Frieda decided to bust through the locked door of the Saloon and take her place behind the bar again. They'd been gathering there nearly every night ever since. They had formed their own little tribe now, The People Who Stayed, and if they had enough liquid reinforcement to pretend things were normal, if they could fool themselves into believing it was just another Saturday night at the Chico Saloon, then maybe they could make it through another day.

Frieda made sure everyone had a full beer, and then she stepped on stage with her acoustic guitar. It had been ages since a band played at the Saloon. She missed the raucous crowds that used to pack this bar, the laughing and dancing and shouting, the rollicking music that rocked this place. But there was no electricity for amps and mics anymore, and not many bands wanted to travel to a Superfund site to play for an audience in the single digits.

Frieda strummed a series of mournful minor chords, and everyone looked her way. She closed her eyes and sang, her deep bluesy voice rumbling through the room like thunder. She repeated the words "cool clear water" over and over again, and everyone sat rapt as they listened to the rhythmic chant, their mouths hanging open and their eyes glistening in the candlelight. Each syllable pulsed through the blood and bones of the tiny audience, a powerful anthem to all they had lost: "cool clear wa-ter, cool clear wa-ter, cool clear wa-ter."

After Frieda plucked the final note from her guitar, she looked around the room. Mike was leaning low over the bar, his nose almost touching the polished wood.

Kim's hands came together in a slow, quiet clap that quickly died to silence. Harold had a faraway look in his eyes, as if he were lost in another time and place altogether.

They were all told the water was safe after the Accident. Harold drank the water. His late wife drank the water. The little kids who lived next door drank the water. Harold continued irrigating until his fields shriveled to dust, the native bunchgrass giving way to patchy stands of cheatgrass and knapweed. The gophers disappeared first, and then he stopped hearing the coyotes yipping just out of rifle range as the sun went down. The elk moved on to better pastures. His cattle started wasting away, their protruding ribs a slap in the face every time he walked outside. Then his wife got sick. He watched as everything his family had worked for over the last hundred years crumbled to nothing. The bank sent threatening letters. "They can't take my land from me! It's mine!" he yelled to anyone who would listen, his face reddening and his voice rising to a desperate pitch. But of course they could, and they did. He would have given anything for cool clear water in those final days.

Frieda returned to the bar and refreshed everyone's beers. The room was subdued, everyone lost in the bittersweet memories that lingered in the silence. Mike lost the battle with gravity and had collapsed over the bar with his eyes closed and his mouth sagging open, a dribble of drool bubbling at the corner of his lips with each rattling breath. He hadn't had a haircut since the Accident, and his straggly hair and bushy beard made him look like a feral animal sleeping beside them. He came to life when he heard the bottles being opened, pushing himself a few inches off the bartop and reaching for another beer.

Harold suddenly leaped from his barstool. "What's that?" he said, his voice sharp and eager as a child's.

"What?" Kim said.

"That's ... I think that's ..." Harold cocked his head with a quizzical look on his face, and then he jogged toward the back door. Kim followed, and Frieda walked quickly behind them.

As soon as they stepped outside, Frieda heard the crescendo of wild voices rising around them. The piercing howls echoed over the land, rolling down through the grassy hills to the river and reverberating off the mountaintops, an eerie song hurtling through the night sky with such primal energy that it seemed to electrify everything around them.

Frieda's body tingled from her hair down to her toes. Moonlight washed over the bruised land, gilding everything with a silvery light. Kim's eyes sparkled, and fifty years seemed to fall from Harold's face. There was a time Harold would have grabbed a gun at the sound of a wolf pack, but now his hands hung limp and open. They all knew that if there were wolves, there must be some furred or feathered prey moving through this drainage again. The right side of Harold's mouth curled up in a lopsided grin.

Then a tremulous howl rose behind them, lonely, mournful, yearning. Frieda turned and saw Mike standing in the doorway, his head thrown back and one hand wrapped tightly around his Trout Tears, a long keening wail coming out of him as if that wild cry had been locked inside him for a thousand years: *Arrooooooh!*

When Mike finally quieted, he stood slack and spent in the moonlight. They all held their breath through the long silence that followed, and then the wolves answered him, closer now, almost close enough to touch.

Beartooth Rondeau

poetry by Tami Haaland

We don't know whether it's a deer trail
or one made by humans. And the pale
light suspended in the day's drizzle
makes it difficult to tell time, wrestle
ourselves back, or accept that we may fail

to find our way. On the plateau, the stale
smell of scummy ponds, surface-shine thick
with moss, leads to hills we can't seem to scale.
We hardly know

what's right. Dense brush ruffles your hair, a stick
against my shoulder seems likely to impale
this breezy shirt. We're left with a pastel
horizon, misdirection. Look, how this story fizzles
and loses focus. Where to find wind for this sail?
I hardly know.

The Astringent Creek Grizzly
fiction by Doug Peacock

LIFE SHIFTS RAPIDLY for the three grizzlies in the year following the great fires. They emerge from their den in April. Food isn't a problem because so many elk and bison died during the winter. The wild fires stressed these grazing animals and they winterkilled in large numbers.

It is their mother who acts differently. She doesn't seem interested in the sort of play and wrestling in which the family has so often engaged. Her selective aggressiveness toward other bears, which the ferocious sow used to defend her helpless yearling last fall, is now on hold; she retreats subordinately when bigger bears come around, yielding up an elk carcass and moving on to the next. And she is downright grouchy toward her two-year olds.

By late May, the adult bear is actively running off her young; she snarls, bites and chases them away. The two subadults sit on a sagebrush covered knoll, puzzled, and watch their mother graze from two hundred yards away. They don't dare come closer.

The little bears gradually realize that they are on their own when a threatening big male comes courting their mother. They move off, wary of bigger bears during the breeding season. Despite his scarred rear foot that he severely burned in the great fire of 1988, brother bear ambles with just the trace of a limp. Traveling long distances is more of a problem.

The two-year-old grizzlies feed, play and bed together for six more weeks. The sow disappears up Astringent Creek. In July, the twins follow their mother's old trail down to Yellowstone Lake. The male has trouble keeping up. They interrupt their journey to nibble fresh grass growing in the burns. Despite last year's fires, the spawning creeks run clear. Bears have gathered there but the fishing is poor. The subadults probe the local social hierarchy; they interact with the other grizzlies. They find their status enhanced by working as a unit; together, they are able to dominate solitary bears and displace them from the better fishing sites. Sister bear seems precociously aggressive for a grizzly of scant 200 pounds.

The inseparable union of the two-and-a-half-year-old grizzlies uncouples on the shores of the great lake. Sister bear wants to follow her mother's footprints back into the high country. Her brother knows the abrasive, angular scree of the Absoroka Range will be too sharp for his scarred paw. Nearby, grow abundant yampa, grass and still-edible forbs; he can also dig for rodents and ants without trekking far. Sister grizzly hangs out with her brother for two days digging roots, then reluctantly, departs alone for the high ridges. The only anxious moment comes when she must cross the road. The bear remembers the traumatic encounter with the tall man. She sits watching the traffic for an hour. The grizzly smacks her lips and pops her jaw; she seems agitated. Suddenly, she darts across the highway, into the trees and up the mountain.

Climbing up into the mountains, the young female from Astringent Creek passes through a square-mile patch of burned trees. The grass is just coming up here. She stops to graze, stepping on mushrooms. There are thousands of morels, false morels, early boletus and countless other fungi popping up everywhere in the burn. She samples them, wolfing down a few morels, then settling on a coarse gilled mushroom that resembles the kind that her mother preferred. She eats a bellyful.

On the talus slopes, the bear finds few cutworm moths this year. But the whitebark pine trees—the ones that survived the fire—are loaded with cones. She feeds on the caches of squirrels for the next month. Other grizzlies pass through. One day she spots her mother raking pinecones a quarter mile away, on the north flank of Cathedral Peak.

The young grizzly, now a luxurious light brown silvertip in the amber sunshine of autumn, begins a unique passage in her life. For much of the next year, she will shadow her mother, tagging behind at a respectful distance, but very much within the sphere of influence of the older female. The instruction will continue.

In the wake of the great fire, the whitebark pine trees sag under the weight of a huge cone crop. The pine nuts provide abundant fat for that fall and the following spring. The rich, concentrated food allowed the thirteen year-old bear to tolerate other grizzlies who fed nearby and probably opened the window to the renewed relationship with her weaned two-year-old.

When the sow moves east to den on Stonecrop Mountain, the younger bear trails just a few hundred feet behind. Both are fat. The smaller grizzly weighs well over 200 pounds and her mother a hundred more. The mother has a den already prepared near the old site. Sister bear pokes around and tentatively starts excavating rocks at the foot of dead tree a quarter mile downhill of her mother's den. Snow flurries encourage her to dig faster. By the time the blizzard arrives, the subadult lies snug in her grass bed at the end of the four-foot tunnel.

§

In mid-April, the three-year-old female spots her mother leaving the den site with three tiny new cubs. All five bears head down Astringent Creek, the family roaming three hundred yards in advance of the solitary grizzly. The two bigger bears seem comfortable with this degree of separation. Throughout the spring, the sow with the three little brown cubs is seen feeding or nursing within a quarter mile of a light brown subadult grizzly.

The extended bear family embarks on a journey over the deep snows into the whitebark pine forests. Travel is not too difficult as long as the snow holds a crust and the bears can walk on top. The smaller female watches while her mother sniffs out the caches of red squirrels now buried under four feet of snow. The sow reaches down and claws out the cones. Soon, the subadult figures out the technique and excavates caches on her own. The cone production the previous fall was enormous; there are still a lot of nuts left for the bears.

She watches as her mother nurses the three new cubs. The weather warms up. The sow departs the high country for the big valley; the afternoon snow is too soft to hold the cubs up. The three-year-old bear lingers for a week and loses track of her mother. No matter, the young female is doing fine on her own. She will find the older bear back on this mountain come autumn.

September rolls around. A dusting of fresh snow

crowns the higher peaks. Five bears amble over the alpine tundra. Mother bear leads her three new cubs into a mountain pass. The young female from Astringent Creek, now at 250 pounds, trails a hundred yards behind. In the autumnal sunlight, she looks increasingly tan and sports a silver-haired collar behind her hump, much like her mother.

The bears travel east down a long valley into the National Forest. During morning and evening, gunshots reverberate up and down the beautiful drainage. It is big game hunting season. The younger grizzly has never been down here before; she wonders why her mother is taking the gamble—the depletion of the over-wintered pinecone caches, the failure of the whitebark crop this year? It defies everything the mother grizzly has taught her: that almost every human is dangerous, that the ones with rifles are the most deadly and that humans in the National Forest are not the same as those in the National Park. These two-legged predators should be avoided at all cost.

But mother bear and her cubs have nutritional needs far beyond what the younger female can comprehend. The rifle shots mean elk carcasses and gut-piles. They need the food. She must risk it.

The grizzlies slink through the gathering shadows. Sticking to the timber, they bypass horse corals and clusters of wall-tents with loud people and barking dogs. Sister bear is nervous and follows her mother reluctantly. It is getting dark.

Shots explode in a nearby meadow. The hunters have killed a bull elk. One man pulls out a knife and begins butchering. He pulls out a pile of intestines. The other hunters twist fearfully in their saddles, checking out the gloomy forest for creatures of the night.

The three men abandon the elk, making no effort to cut it up or drag it off. They ride off to camp.

The bears go to work. The two bigger grizzlies rip open the carcass and feed for two hours. Mother bear drags the huge elk almost to the tree line. They eat again and the sow covers the dead ungulate with sticks and dirt. They bed in the timber two hundred feet away.

The five grizzlies are brutally awakened by gunshots and snarling dogs. The appropriation of the elk has made the hunters angry and they fire blindly into the trees. Bullets crash through the underbrush. The sow makes no move to defend the carcass; she flees into the forest with her three cubs close behind. The subadult bear runs for her life. The men incite the dogs to join the chase, urging them on, shooting over their heads into the timber. The canine pack closes in on the family and snags one cub by the leg. The dogs tear into the little bear. The sow turns to fight them off and takes a .243 slug in the hip. She limps off with her two other offspring. The remaining cub is ripped to pieces by the dogs. The men on horseback gather around and watch them finish off the tiny bear.

The three-and-a-half-year-old grizzly covers the entire distance back to the Yellowstone divide in a few hours. She will not find her mother. Her maternal education is complete.

The cycle begins again. The Astringent Creek Grizzly roams the old family homestead with cubs of her own. The two little bears constitute her second litter. This 350-pound sow has attained a high and legendary status among the grizzlies of interior Yellowstone—as a fiercely protective mother toward other bears and as a discriminating force to be reckoned with by humans. She is now almost the same age as her own mother was when she first trailed mom into the valley as a cub.

A thin, jagged scar runs from her left eye down her snout. One ear wears a deep notch. This combative disfigurement is unusual in a female grizzly. Older boars are normally the ones carrying wounds from challenges by other males during the breeding season. The female from Astringent Creek is exceptional; all other bears know of her ferociousness in defending her cubs or a hoard of food.

With people, she is more cautious. She is aware that humans in Yellowstone Park are largely benign compared to the gun-toting killers in the National Forest. But part of grizzly aggression is innate, a reflexive response to threats to her cubs. Whenever possible she avoids the two-legged mammals. But during the summer, they go everywhere. Worst of all, people behave unpredictably when they see a bear. Sometimes, when she is sleeping on a daybed, they have gotten much too close.

Once, she made physical contact not far from the Pelican Valley trailhead. The Astringent Creek Grizzly was digging roots in a finger meadow separated from the hiking trial by a fringe of trees. Two cubs trailed behind her. As the early summer day warmed, the family ambled toward the trees to bed, crossing the trail on the way.

As soon as she reached the human pathway she saw them coming. Two garishly clad people were running down the trail straight into the grizzly family. The two joggers skidded to a stop thirty feet from the agitated sow. The man in the lead froze at the side of the wide path. The man behind turned and broke into a run. The bear charged past the man standing in the trail, almost brushing him aside, in pursuit of the fleeing jogger. Just as she closed on the man, he hit the ground and lay still. The sow stopped on top of him, straddling his leg with her forepaws. The man didn't move. The bear sniffed the man, but didn't touch him. She spun as the other jogger took advantage of the five-second pause to sprint down the trail in the opposite direction, directly past her cubs. In a heartbeat, the bear was upon him, knocking him to the ground, standing directly over him ready to deliver a killing bite to his head. At the last microsecond, she hesitated; her jaws closed an inch from the man's skull. The sow rested one paw on the jogger's shoulder and turned back to check on her cubs; they cowered beside the trail. Neither human stirred. The big grizzly bolted back and gathered her cubs, all three running off into the timber. The man was unhurt. The bear anticipated the armed rangers who indeed came looking for her. But she was long gone.

[Excerpted from *The Essential Grizzly*. Globe Pequot, 2006.]

Circling Back
essay by Charlotte McGuinn Freeman

ON A BRIGHT MORNING IN MID-JUNE, my sweetheart and I drive across the county to a burn, one that went wild the summer before. A controlled burn, the Forest Service folks call them, but all too often, like most things in the natural world, the fire escapes human control. Chuck and his buddy Keith watched the smoke go up from the cabin they were working on and he took note, knowing that morels love a burn, and this one, in a remote corner of the county, was likely to be forgotten by spring.

We get to the trailhead, relieved to see it empty. We try to get out mid-week when we can, to avoid running into people. We're spoiled by the ratio of space to people in Montana. It's not unusual to find only a single car, maybe two at a trailhead, but since we're mushroom hunting today, we're thrilled that no one else is up here.

Here in Paradise Valley we live surrounded by moun-

132

tain ranges, wilderness areas and Yellowstone National Park, but just as important are all the other state and federal lands on the borders of those areas. We're hunting mushrooms on the national forest, on a maintained trail that I'm sure, if we followed it far enough would lead us up into the Beartooth Absaroka Wilderness Area. We might be outside the wilderness area, but we're still in wild country, and it's these buffer areas, the ones that absorb the brunt of the recreation and hunting pressure, that are all too often overlooked in discussions about conservation and preservation.

The two mining operations that currently threaten the health of our wild country are in these buffer areas, and in previously mined areas. But while mining might have spawned our state nickname, over the past few decades, tourism and recreation have surpassed the extractive mining and timber industries. We are now an economy largely dependent on the nature of our nature, one of the last places in America where you can drive to a trailhead and your chances of having a peaceful day in the woods to yourself are pretty good.

I moved to Montana in 2002, largely because I could access a wealth of trails a short drive from town. I've lived in cities, New York, San Francisco, Chicago, Salt Lake, but I've never lasted long in any city where I couldn't find a trail I could walk every day that would get me out of the buildings, and back into nature. Here, I walk the trails with my dog, and usually prefer a trail I've walked so often I know it's contours by feel. On my own, I want an hour in the woods, walking and getting some fresh air and letting my dog do doggy things while I think, and dream, and look at birds.

But Chuck hates a trail. When the two of us go out together, we get off-trail as soon as possible, head up some drainage to an elevation where we can see the country, or have gotten far enough back to where the country gets feral. Then we'll slow way down, start to look for things, antlers and mushrooms and signs of animals.

Chuck hates trails for the same reason he hates most television shows. The experience is wholly mediated. There's no surprise on the trail. The narrative of your experience has been set by the folks who built it, who placed the logs to reduce erosion, who built the little bridges over creeks so you don't get your feet wet. You only see what the trail wants you to see. When I guided rafts in North Carolina all those years ago, we routinely had guests who thought that our trip was, like the one at Dollywood over the hill, on tracks. "You got a bear?" they'd ask. "At Dollywood they've got a bear. It jumps out at you." No, we explained, usually while doing the safety talk. The rafts weren't on tracks. You had to pay attention. We don't have a mechanical bear. To Chuck, this is how a trail feels, like a raft on tracks.

That day though, we had a mission, finding mushrooms, so we stuck to the trail for the hour or so it took to access the burn. Once the forest opens up we can see where the fire swept through. The ground is black, but the aspens have that electric-green look they get when they've first leafed out, and despite the ash and char, grass and flowers and huckleberries seem already to be taking root. We veer off into the burn, slowing down and spreading out. Chuck puts a finger to his lips, whispers that we might see bears, and I nod that I will try to restrain my usual crowing over mushrooms.

Mushrooming brings out the competitor in me. When we'd first started dating, he took me out along the ditch behind his cabin. The first morel I saw, I splashed right through the water in my Chuck Taylors making "ooh! ooh!" noises as I went. As if it was going to get away. It was a nice one, a big fat black morel popping up through the grass underneath an aspen stand. Hunting morels is like that. I want the first one. I want to find more of them than he does. I can't help but watch his bag and compare it to mine as we hike.

To an easterner, Montana looks huge and empty, but those of us who live here know it's more complicated than that. We share these mountains with all sorts of creatures, from squirrels and foxes all the way up the food chain to bears, wolves and mountain lions. We also share these mountains with other humans. It is not uncommon to see bootprints even in drainages way off the trail, especially when mushroom hunting. We get to the beginning of the burn and are thrilled to see that the only bootprints are old, and mostly Chuck's from when he scouted up here a week ago.

But there's always our non-human neighbors to consider. There are both grizzly and black bears, and we're careful to keep our wits about us. There's no reason to be hysterical about bears. It's like anything in the wilderness—you have to pay attention. When you're off the trail, you need to watch the sun, check landmarks, keep your sense of direction, look up often to see what is in the woods with you.

With bears, there are two schools of thought about how to proceed in the woods. One school advocates making a lot of noise so the bears know you're there. This is what the experts advise for visitors, the use of bells on packs, loud discussion, sticking to the trail, traveling in groups. If you don't have much experience in the woods, or with wild animals, this makes sense. But there's another school, one that advocates being quiet, and paying close attention to terrain and scat and time of day. The danger with any wild animal comes when you surprise it. Bears respond to surprise with attack, and that they're fully capable of doing serious harm to humans is something to take seriously. These are real mountains that contain real dangers, they're not just a scenic backdrop. Chuck belongs to the second school of thought, and over the years he's been rewarded by the sight of several bears, as well as wolves and elk, and moose, and bison.

For me, it comes down to a question of perspective. Are you going into the woods to participate, or are the woods simply backdrop to your all-important human experience? If you're going out there to participate, if you want to see what's there, if you want to let it in rather than impose your viewpoint all over the landscape, then you'll want to be quiet, you'll want to look around, you'll want to enter as you would someone else's house, with respect, with some manners.

The first time Chuck and I went on a hike, we came across a grizzly. We were walking along a green spring hillside and I was looking at the shaggy Icelandic ponies on the other side of the barbed wire when he stopped, put a finger to his lips, motioned to get down. We crouched. He pointed downhill toward the bear. It was definitely a grizzly. It wasn't a huge grizzly, but he wasn't a cub either—a subadult, maybe five years old?

He was down in the creek bed, digging up some kind of bulbs or tubers and eating them. While it's hard to say exactly, he was maybe fifty yards away. Close enough that if he'd taken a notion to, he could have loped up the hill and swatted us with his giant claws in less time than it would have taken to drop and hide under our insufficient daypacks. Chuck pulled his binoculars out, very slowly. I unzipped the compartment on my pack where the bear spray lives as quietly as I could and pulled it out.

"Look," he whispered handing the binocs to me. "You can see his gleaming incisors."

We hadn't been going out that long, and I wanted to seem like a good sport, so I looked, but all I could envision was the binoculars filling up with charging grizzly, so I handed them back. I didn't want to see his gleaming incisors. I wanted to see all of him, downhill, grazing quietly, huge and powerful and not charging us.

Chuck would look for a while, then hand them to me. I'd pretend to look, terrified that moving would attract the bear's attention, then hand them back. Mostly, I peeked at the bear over Chuck's shoulder. He was beautiful, and I can't imagine that he didn't know we were there. But he didn't seem to care about us, lying at the top of the hill, watching him. It was spring, and he was a bear, and there were tubers, and he was going to keep digging them up for as long as he kept finding them. And so we watched, and waited, and passed the binoculars back and forth, all the while marveling that there was a real, live, wild grizzly bear *right there*, doing his grizzly bear thing.

§

Back in the burn hunting morels, it happens, that magic moment where suddenly you see mushrooms everywhere that you'd have sworn weren't there two seconds ago. "Aha!" I mutter, pouncing. Morels. They're not huge, but they are plentiful, especially in the burned-out hollows left from the roots of trees. I scurry from one clump to another, rooting around in the soot. Then I come across a bear scat. It is very fresh. It is also very small. This is not a good sign. That means there's a cub in the neighborhood. Which means there's a mama. I point it out to Chuck, who points to the mama bear scat he's just passed. We look around, but don't see anything, and so we keep going.

I look at his mushroom bag. We're about even.

§

That first time we went hiking, we watched the bear for probably ten minutes before he finally ambled off down the drainage. It was thrilling. Terrifying, but thrilling. Once he'd ambled through the copse of trees downstream from where he'd been grazing, once we'd watched him cross the grassy meadow and disappear into the forest, I stood up, still a little trembly from the excitement of it all, stretched my creaky knees and said "Well that's too bad."

"What do you mean?" Chuck asked.

"We're going back to the car," I said. "Aren't we?"

"No," he said, as if I was loony. "The bear went that way," he pointed down the drainage. "And we're going across and up that way. We're fine. We know where he is."

I looked at him. We were still going in there? Really? I looked up at the dark forest covering the mountainside in front of us. It looked like the forest primeval out of Grimm.

Then I glanced over at the Icelandic ponies. They were grazing as though nothing had happened. I grew up around horses, and they're notoriously panicky. If the ponies weren't spooked, I decided that meant they knew that bear, which meant that bear lived here, which meant that somehow this crazy person I was with might be right. The bear was going about his business. We knew where he was and we weren't going to bother him.

Chuck stood there waiting for me to make up my mind. "Um," I said putting my day pack back on. "Okay, I guess." And then, clutching my bear spray, I followed him downhill to where the bear had been. We admired his enormous paw prints, ogled the wide claw marks, and then I followed Chuck across the stream, and up into the woods.

§

We live in one of the rare places where human beings are not the apex of the food chain. We live in a place where there are a lot of things that human beings are hardwired to fear: darkness, wolves, grizzly bears, mountain peaks, freak snowstorms, lightning, avalanches, mushrooms. All of these can kill you—sometimes even when you do everything right. It's what I love about wild country.

The first year I lived here, my beloved younger brother died in a car crash. I was a wreck, and I survived it largely by walking. I walked my dogs up either Suce or Pine Creek once a day, often weeping silently behind my sunglasses. One evening, about a year after Patrick died, the dogs and I were strolling along, when I heard a weird, loud, repeated CHUFF. I came into the clearing and saw a bear, standing on his hind legs at the top of the game trail. Time slowed down the way it does when your adrenalin kicks in. I called the dogs, who were young then and not particularly obedient, but there must have been something in my voice, that tone you use when a kid is running into traffic, and they came back, came and heeled. I'd just read Scott McMillion's *Mark of the Grizzly*, and as I held out my bear spray, I remember thinking, *what did Scott say to do?* The bear was enormous, standing on his hind legs, peering at us with his tiny little eyes, and even through my terror I thought, *Great, after the year I've had? Now I'm going to have my scalp ripped off?* Clutching the bear spray in front of me, I treated the bear like a big, angry drunken man. "Nice bear," I said quietly, as we backed away, out of the clearing, back into what felt like the safety of the trees. "Sorry bear. We're leaving bear. Didn't mean to bother you bear." I didn't look directly at him, but didn't turn my back on him either. The dogs were puzzled and clueless, but stayed by my side until we climbed up out of the drainage, up into the sweet little meadow that looks west over Paradise Valley and the Gallatin range, where I had to sit on a rock to get over the adrenaline shakes.

Many of us are drawn to these wild landscapes *because* we're a little scared. Facing fear, managing it, deciding what risk you're going to take then walking into it, this holds out the promise of a real experience, one that *requires* that you wake up, that you pay attention. When Chuck and I hike in bear country, we carry bear spray, and we keep our voices down, and we stop often to look and listen to what is going on around us. We are very much alive, and alert, and engaged. So much so that those times we've been hiking in other parts of the state, places where there are only black bears, but not grizzlies, it feels a little flat, a little boring.

So far, we haven't had any unpleasant encounters with wild animals. What we have had are moments like the one watching that bear forage, or finding wolf tracks when we went to cut a Christmas tree, or finding a rocky cove where it was clear from the bone evidence that wolves had been using the landscape as a sort of trap for elk and deer, driving them into a cul-de-sac where they were easier to kill. However, just because we haven't had trouble with wild animals doesn't mean we're doing it right, or that I'd tell you to approach wild country the way we do. We might just have been lucky.

It's like anything, it's like love itself, you assess the territory, you note your vulnerability and level of risk, and then you nod, put your pack back on, and walk down the hill, across the creek and into the woods.

That spring day up in the burn, we hunted morels through a lovely soft rain. We crossed the burn, working our way slowly uphill, from morel patch to morel patch, then crossed a rock reef and descended back down into the forest again. We never did see any bears, which was fine with me, although we did see a very festive striped skunk who waved his big white tail while he scurried along the gully bottom below us. At day's end, Chuck had slightly more morels than I did, but not by much. And anyway, after about three hours of wandering in the woods, I go into an endorphin fog where my competitive nature melts away, and I'm happy just to be out in the woods, walking along.

Circling back that afternoon, Chuck and I came upon a small creek that fell from mossy pool to mossy pool down the side of the mountain. It was only a trickle back in the woods, the kind of beauty we would never have found if we hadn't gone off the trail. And then we climbed back up, out of the mossy bottomland, found the trail again and drove home, where we feasted on sautéed morels on pasta, and slept the sleep of people who have walked outside in the fresh air and the rain all day.

The opportunity to engage with the wild world, to go out into nature where you do not know what you will encounter, is a resource that is growing scarce. There will always be a huge majority who simply drive through Yellowstone, drive up Highway 89 looking at our beautiful mountains, at the Yellowstone River flowing free along the valley bottom. And yet, in some of those cars are kids who have seen a real mountain for the first time, a real river, perhaps even glimpsed a bear along the way, the kind of kids who will go home as I did all those decades ago and dream of big landscapes, dream until they're old enough to come out here. We owe it to those kids to preserve the wild nature we so love, to declare it more valuable than one more mine.

Just Now Beginning

poetry by Joan Kresich

Visiting friends want to know which animals
they will see.
I try to explain what has taken me, bred on city
sidewalks, so long to learn.
We won't know which animals will appear, or
where or when. Opening wide
our senses like infants just arriving, we'll give our
eyes free rein and find
they're hungry for the journey to the horizon,
our ears rising to track
muffled sounds.

And then, as though all life were just now
beginning, a fox will emerge
from the dark fringes onto the sleeping-snow
meadow. She'll lift each foot
in the cadence of her clan, and behind her a trail
of prints will lengthen in an arc.
Her fur will be a great gathering of warmth, rust
and red, brown and tan and bits
of black. At the very moment when it seems there
is nothing more to ask
another fox will break free of darkness on the
other side. The two
will bring their arcs to meet and in one supple
moment
their moist black noses will meet.

Mountain Road

poetry by Ilona Popper

17 below this morning

the fox started running
from the ridge
as if she needed
that head start to beat my car
and she made it
ahead of my four wheels
my red metal sides
barely panting
as she stood on the other bank
but I pulled over
just to look and
she jumped out of sight
hearing the great noise
of my compact car
angle in towards her

back home
on my cell
I looked through the window
and saw another fox
on the dirt road
tail out and
coat fluffed up to trap the heat
trotting like a neighbor's dog
Amex
I said into the cell

number 841 9191...
clamped the phone between my jaw and ear
grabbed the camera
looked again for that
hot red ashy hunter
black ears
my finger pressed *on*
four black legs
expiration 4/18 I said to
the customer service representative
while he
leaped through the barbed wire
into the field
what? I said *oh yeah*
the confirmation number
but I
stepped on the porch
camera in one hand
cell in the other
he turned his face
eyes slits rimmed black
zoom zoom
the camera said
pale orange cheeks
zoom zoom
the fox in the view screen
pounced and shook his coat

when I looked up
from the screen
he stared me down
kabuki frown
fear curving his eyes
my email address?

147

I said to the cell
he jerked his head away
just as I took the shot

you know you can't catch a fox
that way

no way to catch
a fox

now the stars burn by the millions
above where I stand
hopping in the dark
to bear the bitter cold
so I might hear if the wolf
speaks again tonight

Natural Instinct
essay by Seabring Davis

SIXTEEN YEARS AGO, I hiked into Emigrant Gulch when I was nine months pregnant. I did not know about motherhood yet, about its fleet changes, nor the deep instincts it would rile in me. I didn't know that Emigrant Gulch held a great lesson that day.

It was October and hot for that time of year in Montana. My friend Carter drove over from Bozeman to take in the rare lingering autumn of Paradise Valley. We met at Chico Hot Springs Resort, hopped into my blue Jeep Wrangler and bounced up the county road toward the trailhead. Passing through the historic gold mining settlement of Old Chico we turned left where the dirt road narrows and runs by homesteads-turned-summer-cabins. Our dogs whined with anticipation for the hike. Between us there were three: Carter's faithful yellow Lab, and my two, a German Shepherd and a black Lab mix.

149

When the road got rough enough to threaten a flat tire, I parked near the bridge over Emigrant Creek. Ours was the only car at the trailhead. The dogs were in a frenzy of barks and yips, scratching at the door to be let loose. When I opened the hatch of the Jeep they burst out in three different directions, noses to the ground, inhaling the scents of the trail.

We laughed at their exuberance, but I felt almost as excited. After a lengthy doctor-prescribed bedrest, it was my first hike in two months. Late afternoon sun filtered through yellowing leaves of ripe chokecherry bushes. The spiny branches of lodgepole pines hung with pale green moss on either side of the creek where the trail forks. Across the bridge a rocky mining road leads deep into the Gulch. The area has a complicated land use history dating back to the 1860s when gold was discovered in the creek and the hardiest of settlers staked claims. Before then, it was Crow territory. Before the gold rush, no one owned this land. I would argue that no one ever truly can. Emigrant Peak towers protectively, its base stepped high with black volcanic talus.

Carter and I chose the left fork, a gentler and shorter route that leads to a waterfall. The dogs rushed ahead, chasing squirrel chatter that was lost in Emigrant Creek's echo off the canyon walls. Even that late in the year, the flow was still strong. We raised our voices to hear each other over the creek, walking and talking. We passed one last cabin and a dozen no-trespassing signs, dimpled with bullet holes.

As we hiked, Carter generously listened to my pregnancy woes. My fears of the changes to come and my prattling about baby names. At 29 I'd struggled with the inevitable transformation I felt happening. The body changes. The weight gain. The need for rest. The way my life would eminently shift after the baby was born. The way it seemed to have already changed.

Before I found out about the pregnancy, I'd been training for a marathon-length trail run in the Bridger Mountains, a goal I had wanted to achieve before turning 30. I kept running even after I found out I was pregnant, but it hadn't been easy. At seven months, when my belly bulged to the size of a watermelon, I could no longer see my feet strike the trail. I had to rely on the shuddering sensation that moved through my whole body. But I kept logging miles, walking when I felt off balance. I was determined to finish that race.

In August the labor pains started. It was too early. My official due date was Halloween. After a day of pain, I went to visit my doctor. In the exam room at the hospital he palpated my abdomen and inquired about my activity. His eyes were stern.

"I haven't let the pregnancy interfere with my training, but I'm taking it easier," I said. The week before I'd logged 25 trail miles, easily under the average number needed to legitimately train for a 23-mile race at 10,000-feet elevation. He nodded and continued my exam.

"I eat well," I added defensively, "and get lots of sleep." More nodding. "Pregnancy isn't a disability!" My voice was shrill. He met my eyes, then turned and left the room. The nurse told me to get dressed.

A few minutes later he knocked, then opened the door. He sat on a short, rolling stool; the nurse stood against the wall, smiling. I sat on the exam table. My feet dangled over the edge like a child's.

High blood pressure had caused premature labor, as well as sharp, needle-like pains in my arms and legs. My feet were so swollen that the only shoes that would fit them were my husband's size-ten Nikes. The fetus was under duress, the doctor said. And it was my fault. He told me to stop working. And to stop running.

I started to cry. "Why should pregnancy change the way I live?"

At this point my doctor rolled in closer. He took my hand and asked if I wanted to go into premature labor on a mountain ridge. Without cell service. Even if there was cell service, he said, and I was able to reach 9-1-1, would the emergency responders be there in time to help me? And *if* they were able to reach me by helicopter while I labored at 8,600 feet on a ridge with no shade or water, did I really want my child to be born like that?

None of this had occurred to me. I had only been thinking of my own desire to finish some arbitrary race, to prove that I was in control, that having a baby didn't make me old. I kept crying, but now out of shame.

He patted my hand and rolled his stool backward. "You won't be pregnant forever," he said.

Reluctantly, I ended my training. The pains stopped, the swelling lessened. Finally, in October, nearing my due date, the doctor said little walks were safe again. I ached to be on a trail, far from the town noises of neighbors, trains and summer traffic.

Though Emigrant Gulch is not far from the bustle of Chico or from the tourist traffic headed to Yellowstone National Park's northern entrance, relatively few people access the trails here. Even fewer venture into the adjacent Absaroka-Beartooth Wilderness. I like to remember that some of the oldest known rocks have been found in the Absaroka Mountains, dating back 49 million years. The fact makes me feel small, but also connected to these greater mountains that stretch across Montana and Wyoming. I like knowing that it's habitat for wolves, bears, mountain lions. Despite its natural beauty, the area has been continually encroached by mining ventures, proposals for real estate expansion and recreational use.

Even still, it remains wild.

Carter shared my love for hiking. We had news to catch up on as we walked up the shaded trail. Blissfully unattached and childless, I loved listening as she recounted road trips, new jobs and new lovers. She seemed fearless and free, pushing ahead with a life full of opportunity. Vicariously, I absorbed and envied her single-girl adventures.

Before long, we arrived at the little falls just above a wooden footbridge. The Balm of Gilead Creek, just a tiny line on a topo map, that in real time cascades over electric green algae-covered rocks, watercress patches and deadfall before it meets with the bigger flow of Emigrant Creek.

Who gave this creek its name? Gilead is a biblical reference to peace. I wonder what legacy did he or she hope to leave with this name. The dogs romped through the water, fetching sticks and tussling.

Emigrant Creek starts high up as a trickle from Mineral Mountain. It carves through volcanic rock, into the gulch and sews its stalwart thread along the seam of Emigrant Peak before running into the Yellowstone River. From Emigrant Peak's steeps there are other creeks with names that reflect hard rock miner pipe dreams: Gold Prize, Placer Basin, Gold Run. The whole 7,900 acres of Emigrant Gulch are marked with the claims of mining industry.

The place names up Emigrant Gulch serve as time stamps of history. Originally named for immigrants who settled here in 1863 when gold was discovered. The district is also known as Chico, Curry, Shorthill, Mill Creek, named for prospectors who tried their luck in the early days of Montana Territory. They left names as markers of their labor and hope. Ultimately, the names are all that remain of them, while the mountains and the surrounding wilderness live on.

We didn't stay there for long. The sun had gone down, and the air turned chill. The mood had shifted as the shade in the canyon turned shadowy. Perhaps ghosts of those who named this creek, I mused. Carter and I turned to retrace the trail, taking a quick pace to make the two-and-a-half miles back to the Jeep.

Those early miners spent months deep in the shadows of Emigrant Gulch. They fought the elements and the hostile bands of Crow who attacked their trespassing settlement. Other treasure hunters followed and profited briefly even as recently as 1994. They found gold, copper, silver and other precious minerals. Later it was simply the hard work in the austere terrain that made them lose heart. What remains are the "ghost town" of Yellowstone City, rumors of a lost mother lode and scraps of mining equipment. Even the most historically productive gold mine, St. Julian, is just a pile of remnant logs.

A few minutes down the trail, all three dogs bolted ahead. Surprised, we call them back: *Indi! Stella! Bay! Come!*

They ran at full speed, on the chase, around a bend and out of sight. Carter jogged ahead, I held my enormous belly, walking faster to catch up. The barking echoed off the rock walls. We caught up to them and saw the three dogs standing noses-to-noses with two bear cubs. Nearly as big as the dogs, the cubs were sandy faced, standing their ground in a band of trees abutting a scree-hillside.

Frantically, we recalled the dogs. As the shepherd came to me, one of the cubs ran up the hill. I held Stella's collar, still yelling at the other dog. The second cub scurried up the trunk of a thick Douglas fir out of reach of the Labs. After more barking, Carter's dog ran to her side, trembling with excitement. Finally, my black Lab returned too. We heeled them and quickly turned down the trail, rattled and holding tight to the dogs' collars.

After a few paces, Carter said, "How old do you think those cubs are?" I guessed that they were yearlings. "That means there's probably a mama bear somewhere nearby," she said.

We looked back on the rocky trail. Empty. The creek was hidden by chokecherry-laden bushes. Dusk had settled into the drainage. A bear could be anywhere along our path back to the car; it seemed very likely we were between her and the cubs.

"We need to make a lot of noise," I said, dragging a large branch, easily eight-feet long, from the side of the trail. We moved downhill, Carter and I holding the branch in front of us, horizontally across our chests. The dogs tagged at our heels. I guess the idea was to brandish the branch as a weapon, a jousting lance perhaps that we could thrust toward an enraged bear. We also sang. Loudly.

First, choruses to classic Rock songs: *You can't always get what you want! But if you try sometimes/you get what you need!* And eighties hits: *If you call my name/I will walk on by/ La la lala-la/If you call my name...* Then, because neither of us has a memory for lyrics, nursery rhymes: *Hickory dickory dock! The mouse ran up the clock!*

We moved along this way for two miles, alert and flinching at every rustle of leaves from the evening breeze. We were scared. It felt as if time passed more slowly, making our return seem longer.

It was enough time to reflect on the interaction with the bears and realize how afraid I had been. For myself and my dogs, obviously, but for the first time, too, for my unborn baby. All through my pregnancy I had made those months so hard. I'd struggled to maintain my identity and balked at the physical sacrifices that I could not recognize as so small in the big picture. I recognized I'd been selfish for a very long time. I'd put my child at risk along the way, fighting what was natural and right. In that moment, as we trudged toward safety, Emigrant Gulch, the creek, the peak, the surrounding wilderness, gave me my first lesson of motherhood.

§

Walking, singing, carrying a tree over my pregnant belly for protection it was hard not to admit that there were forces in the world bigger than my own will. That sometimes my own needs must be set aside for a larger purpose. I felt my first instinct to protect myself, my baby and even this place.

I looked up at the slope of Emigrant Peak. The surrounding land is only just recovering from the damage wrought after years of treasure hunting. The craggy road is nearly all that remains of those prospector dreams in Emigrant Gulch. Emigrant and Mineral mountains and this creek still bear their names, but its value is in its wildness. It should remain wild for others to discover that its treasure isn't as tangible as an ounce of gold or a single miner's job. This place is bigger than that.

When we finally reached the Jeep, Carter and I tossed the giant branch to the side of the trail. Exhausted, we loaded the dogs and scrambled into the car. The moment our doors slammed shut, both of us exhaled. Inside the car, we laughed at ourselves. I turned the key in the ignition and we rambled back down the potholed road. We rode home in grateful silence.

A few weeks later on another hike, I went into labor for real. There were no bears this time. There was no race. The hospital was nearby and I gave birth to a healthy baby girl. Today, she walks with me in the shadow of Emigrant Peak.

A Story of Turning Back
essay by Rick Bass

I wonder what Emigrant Peak looks like from the top. It's the dominant feature in Paradise Valley, just outside the historic Chico Hot Springs and just north of Yellowstone National Park. I'm living part of the year a few hundred yards from the mountain's base.

One way to get there: You drive until you can't go any farther. The rocky road up Emigrant Canyon—named for the first wave of miners who came crawling and creeping up this slot in the earth, down which gushes a torrent, a cataract, so narrow that in places a gifted athlete, a single human, could vault from one side to the other without getting wet.

Others, just as resolute, might advance by wading up the creek, slipping on the jagged stones. Tiny crystals glitter here and there like grains of salt drying on a creature's skin, or like scales, or feathers, flexing just-so in the sunlight. *Life*, briefly.

I park and walk. Gutshot spatters of oil—some fresh, others ancient—spackle the cobbles. The road is packed hard by centuries of greed and desperation, but still is loose underfoot—the shards, the puzzle-pieces, will not yet peaceably assemble—and the rubble is treacherous. My ankles tingle. I know how easy it would be to fold or roll one on this infinitude of loose stone.

When you hear the word *treachery*, you think that by virtue of your being aware, you can avoid it: that simple forewarning and awareness are all that's required. But this is not the nature of treachery. Treachery is patient. It waits for you to become fatigued. It waits. In this way it is as patient as geology. It endures, just beneath the surface.

§

Lucky Minerals is the latest to file claims up here. (For God's sake, blokes, at least have some creativity in the naming.) In the old days there were men with mules and pans, bent humpbacked over the torrent, deafened by the incessant roar of the thing they never dreamed might become rare or even go away. Later, here, they dug and scratched, then gouged and blasted. Giant bulldozers clattered and groaned, carving through the seemingly-impossible rock. Once a road is in, in this country, it's all over. It will not be reclaimed. It will not be grown over. It becomes geology. It becomes a way.

161

They came then with giant hoses and vats of acid. There were no rules, and they destroyed much that was beautiful. Then there was one rule, perhaps the most obscene subsidy our country has ever given to industry or the so-called myth of free enterprise and "business." It was the business of wrecking, the business of the 1872 Mining Act, still buried within a dusty quill-and-ink ledger somewhere far in the basement of the Library of Congress. It puts forth a sweet gig for the Canadians—for anyone— where we give up ownership of our mountains to anyone who wants to climb up into the highest points and then stack a little cairn of rocks, plant a little flag. We killed or imprisoned all our native people, shoved them out of these mountains, only to then give the mountains away to any nation who wanted to come in and plant a silly little flag. It's an old rule. There is much in the foundation of our country that is no longer sturdy, if ever it was.

There is much that began wrong, and has not gotten any more right with time. There is much that is great— take the park itself, just a few miles south of here (which was also created in 1872)—but there is also looseness underfoot, and here in Emigrant Canyon, the ghosts, to paraphrase Faulkner, are not even ghosts. The hunger, the meaningless yearning, the hollowness for the colorful mineral, is so profound that it seems you could sift flecks and flakes of it—not the gold, but the wanting, and the

162

unhappiness—from the wild little river with a pan; could distill it, in reverse alchemy, into jewelry or whatnot. Bracelet of sorrow, necklace of regret, amulet of waste and devastation.

Two-thirds of the way up the mountain, there's a new little claim, a scrap of tin, like the scissor-snipped side of soft drink can, the soft metal scratched with a few crude letters, Lucky Minerals, Rosie #22. (Elsewhere, one assumes a Rosie #21, a Rosie #26—maybe half a hundred little Rosie-piles.) There's not even a cairn here, as was done in the old days, no neat stacking of rocks, just some nasty-ass new pink flagging fluttering in the high dry winds aloft, and an empty bottle of pain reliever stobbed onto a branch. *Trash*. Trash. Now they own it, and are presumably waiting, in the time-honored tradition of American kabuki-dance that our government enacts with corporations, to be bought out, paid off, given hundreds of millions of dollars from the federal treasury in exchange for not gouging the gates of Yellowstone further to get to the last and deepest thinleaf sheaf or laminae of gold—the last capillary—that their maps show or prophesy might lie still farther beneath all that has already been sluiced out.

It's like paying someone not to write a novel, or not to embark upon a pro football career. It's damned unlikely that it could be done anyway. But the map proposes value, and Lucky, and Rosie, whoever she is, by sticking her aspirin bottle in the crotch of a tree nearly 10,000 feet above the floor of the old sea (whose trace minerals precipitated out, here and there, falling in slow motion glitter to the bottom of the sea, or circulating deeper within the gurgling fire of the mountains that were about to burst out and be formed), owns this northern gateway to Yellowstone now. Not bad for a day's hike and a penny's worth of plastic flagging. And now Lucky is likely just waiting for Congress to pay them to go away. Holding the mountains hostage.

As if it is still 1872. As if steam vessels are still plying the Atlantic, journeying over from England, as if the Industrial Revolution has not yet begun, as if the Sioux and Cheyenne are still defending this country against the depredation of Custer and the U.S. Army; as if Tolstoy still sits at his desk, writing instead of living a life, as if Einstein is not yet born, is not yet brooding on the equations whose paths will lead to an understanding of how to destroy matter in ways never before imagined. As if Eastern tourists have not even begun to take the long train ride West, braving the wilds of Yellowstone to stuff their dirty laundry down into the pie-hole of Old Faithful, whooping and otherwise exulting when it disgorges long minutes later, steam cleaned, if a bit sulfurous. All gone now, but when the act was written, they were not here yet. They have come and gone, and still the rule remains. You may have our mountains for a song. You may have them for free.

§

Do I pay attention to the artificial, invisible lines of domain? I do not. I travel the shape of the mountain, in violation I suppose, of the 1872 act, written by the same session of Congress that successfully prevented women from voting, and which sought to keep men with non-white skin from voting. The mountain is several hundred million years young, and I walk right up it, picking my way through talus and the shade of droughty overstocked fir, the forest so hot it seems to be panting.

Every step remains treacherous, but I'm distracted. I can't help but look up at the amazing mountains that flank both sides of the canyon. The sweet scent of cottonwoods along Emigrant Creek. Sheer cliffs, single slabs of vertical rock: no way up here, and I walk on, watching, looking for a fissure, a chute. After a few miles there's a gate with a Private Property sign on it, even though the map shows the land belongs to us, to the U.S. government. Public. I've reached Lucky's lode.

Others have been here. Long ago, a pipe was sunk into the ground, up which water wells mysteriously, spreading across the old stone road—a green algae slick of a puddle surrounds the pipe's bubbling mouth, the water is clear, cool, gurgling, tempting, and most assuredly arsenic-laden. I sip from my water bottle, and, to avoid breaching the gate, begin to climb straight up the slope, into the tangled forest, gripping the slender trunks of Doug fir hand over hand.

To my left—in the appropriated territory, or expropriated—the mountain looks pretty lunar: the scene of a mountain massacre. Rubble and rock roads winding and writhing up into a broad basin, the zippered contours of excavations, rumpled hills bulldozer-shoved, terraced troughs dug. It would be nice to take the easier route but the Canadians say they own it now and have posted the hell out of it, telling us we can no longer travel there.

Up through the spindly cliff-clinging trees, then picking a route, straight up. A spine is gained, a fin, which I hope will lead to a ridgeline pass, from which I can then approach the summit of Emigrant.

Altitude is gained: a trade, half a peanut butter sandwich for 500 more feet, or a thousand; a sip of water, clean water, for another 500. After a while I'm high enough to see other scratchings, little human rodent-caves where the miners of a hundred years ago scratched and clawed and sniffed at the rocks like wild beasts in search of salt. It may be assumed they lived quick lives that you might be tempted to say had no real meaning; and you might be right. They could have been mindless machines, not people, searching for any old mindless thing; what did it matter if it had economic worth? They were just scratching at the skin of things, then they left.

Does it matter? Of course it does. Does passion matter? Yes! Isn't obsession one of the peculiar and alluring aspects of being human? Certainly. So why is a passion for digging a claim far up in the lonely, beautiful mountains—and in so doing, using a loophole to wrest control of the ownership of that mountain from the public treasury (350 million of us; one man or woman, one vote)—to one's own brief self—a bad passion? One man or woman, one mountain, now. A mountain in every pot.

Perhaps the differences between good and bad passions, good and bad obsessions, is this: There is that which destroys, and that which builds up or preserves. Perhaps that is all.

There is also I suppose the in-between: the line or path of no-passion, or not-caring. And so the 1872 Mining Act remains, never erased. And our lives are so short and we go on, clinging to the earth for a little while until we fall off, and the torrents and debris, the arsenic and the dust, keep washing down the creek, out to the Yellowstone River, and into time.

§

What a scam. The higher I go, the crosser I get. A mountain is no longer wild when there's a mine on it. A mine kills a mountain. A day of my life has been taken. I chose to climb a wild mountain, but am encountering Rosie's 22nd spoor, Rosie's immortal trash pile. I want my mountain back.

And what of the gold that has been leach-poisoned out of this canyon, and from this mountain, already? Where did it go, and how is the world, or even just our one nation, better for its leaving? At what party was the gold leaf necklace admired; on what beautiful lady, insecure, wanting even more beauty, more youth, when already, now and here, is everything; when the body, bare and alive, young and strong, is so much more than enough?

Essentially this mountain has become a two-bit tattoo parlor, selling the promise of something it can neither sustain nor even deliver.

§

The higher I go, the more brittle the cliffs become: Down lower, there was the steep scree of time-fractured talus; but up higher, the cliffs, rotten with their provenance—ancient sediments lightly lithified, thrust upward and made brittle under pressure—come off in my hand, grip by grip. Boulders tumble down the chutes, clatter and cartwheel sharp-edged, releasing from their broken interiors the acrid scent of rock dust that has not been smelled by any living organism in hundreds of millions of years: dust and air as if from the whirl of a djinn.

These new edges of the cliff are needle-sharp, fang-sharp, and pierce my bare hands; as I ascend, I leave crimson little hieroglyphics on the rocks. Again and again a handhold pulls loose, hurtles down and past my feet, back toward where I started from: as if it is I, and not the miners and their machines, who are dissembling the mountain. As if I am taking it apart stone by stone.

Though I cannot see the top, I can tell I'm getting near the summit by my relative elevation, relative views of the other side of the canyon. And yet: The cliffs are becoming more sheer.

The backside is hard country to traverse. There are 100- and 200-foot spires all around, like those on the churches of the ages, striving upward as if trying to express beauty farther skyward: a church from so long ago. The higher one gets, the more there is to lose. Here and there are avalanche chutes, clefts and fissures barely as wide as my body, chimneys which, though going straight up, do have handholds and footholds. There is a way up; there is a way, as is almost always the case, to keep going forward.

But is it responsible? I have a family to support, and financial obligations. What if I fall and hit my head? I'm climbing solo, without a helmet. Sure, I can go higher, but what if I can't find the same route down, and on the return find myself instead cliffed out, at the edge of a precipice down which there is no safe passage?

And for what?

I make the wise decision and, despite being so near the top, turn around and descend. I'll come back another day and pick another route.

And on my descent, I find the soft rock. It's just to the east, in the mined-over little basin. Of course they claimed the softer, more passable country. Of course they did.

After a while, it appears that I am walking on their land. After a while, it appears that I have crossed some imaginary line, am on a bladed, winding stony road, switchbacking down, down off the mountain, passing more old cairns. Am I on Canadian soil now, I wonder, does Canada own these stones, every one of them?

Many of them are orange and red, others gold, others glow a luminous blue, and still others, black... Quite a few are sulfur-yellow.

Would our country be different if we'd named our first park—the one of which we are most proud, and the one which is most visited, not just by our countrymen and countrywomen, but by all nations—something different? Would we be the same country if we'd named it Bluestone National Park, or Redstone?

No, I don't think so. It's not the same.

Two simple words. *Yellow*, and *stone*.

[Previously published in *Big Sky Journal*, 2016.]

Contributor Bios:

Martha Houston Weaver Adkins, in fifty short years in southern Park County, has odd jobbed her way as ranch hand, painter, cook and finally learned to make a decent apple pie.

Bryce Andrews is the author of *Badluck Way: A Year on the Ragged Edge of the West*. He has worked on and managed cattle ranches in the high, wild valleys of Montana. He lives happily in Missoula, and is writing a second book.

Elise Atchison lives in an off-the-grid cabin on the edge of the Absaroka-Beartooth Wilderness in Montana. Her work has appeared in *Montana Quarterly, South Dakota Review, Silk Road Review, Terrain, Cutthroat Journal, Reflections West Radio*, and elsewhere, and she was awarded a grant from the Barbara Deming Memorial Fund for her forthcoming novel. More at eliseatchison.com.

Rick Bass is the author of over 30 books of environmental essays, novels and short fiction. He has received O. Henry Awards, numerous Pushcart Prizes and fellowships from the National Endowment for the Arts and the Guggenheim Foundation. His latest collection of short stories, *For a Little While*, is a *New York Times Book Review* editor's choice, and he is a board member of the Yaak Valley Forest Council (yaakvalley.org).

Marc Beaudin is the author of *Vagabond Song: Neo-Haibun from the Peregrine Journals,* as well as other books and plays. During the invasion of Iraq, he edited the anti-war anthology *Jihad bil Qalam: To Strive by Means of the Pen*. His work has been seen in numerous journals and is included in the Bangtail Press anthology of Montana writers, *An Elk River Books Reader*. Originally from Michigan, he now lives in Livingston, Montana where he is a bookseller and the artistic director of the Caldera Theatre Company.

Frank Carter grew up in Georgia and Montana. He has years of experience working as an environmental educator, a conservationist, and a writing teacher. Frank earned a master's degree in environmental education from Teton Science School in Kelly, Wyoming and a Master's of science in environmental humanities at the University of Utah. He is a passionate student, naturalist, outdoorsman, author, artist, and musician. He is currently pursuing a master's degree in social work to bridge his conservation and education background with a career in mental health. Frank lives in Bozeman with his wife and son. More at featherbeardmusic.com.

Dave Caserio is the author of *This Vanishing* and *Wisdom For A Dance In The Street*, a CD of poetry and music. A recipient of a Fellowship in Poetry award from the New York State Foundation of the Arts, Dave works with various community outreach programs, Humanities Montana, Arts Without Boundaries, the Billings YMCA/Writer's Voice "Poets on the Prairie" and for the Billings Clinic Cancer Center conducting writing workshops for cancer survivors. He is a founding member of the writer's collective Big Sky Writing, and producer of a series of poetry-in-performance events that combine poetry, music, dance and the visual arts.

John Clayton writes about the history and culture of the American West from his home in Red Lodge. His books include *The Cowboy Girl: The Life of Caroline Lockhart* and, most recently, *Stories from Montana's Enduring Frontier*. A regular contributor to the *Montana Quarterly*, he has also written for *Montana Magazine, Big Sky Journal*, and *High Country News*. His essay included here is taken from a work-in-progress, a cultural history of Yellowstone tentatively titled *Wonderlandscape*. More at johnclaytonbooks.com.

Michael Earl Craig is the current Poet Laureate of Montana. His most recent book of poems is *Talkativeness* (Wave Books, 2014). He is a farrier, and lives in the Shields Valley near Livingston, Montana.

Award-winning journalist **Seabring Davis** is the former editor-in-chief of *Big Sky Journal* and editor emeritus of *Western Art & Architecture*. Her work has been published in *Mountain Living, True West Magazine, Via, Postcards* and *Montana Quarterly*. She is a blogger for TheLastBestPlates.com and the author of five lifestyle books, including, the High Plains Book Award Culinary winner, *A Taste of Montana*, as well as *A Montana Table: Recipes from Chico Hot Springs Resort*.

A fourth generation descendant of Cornish tin miners and Irish copper miners, Butte native **Edwin Dobb** is the co-producer and co-writer of the documentary film *Butte, America*. He writes for *National Geographic, Harper's, Guernica* and other publications, and teaches at the U.C. Berkeley Graduate School of Journalism.

Charlotte McGuinn Freeman is the author of *Place Last Seen*. Since 2002 she has made her home in Livingston, where she gardens, forages for mushrooms and raises backyard chickens. She writes at livingsmallblog.com and other places about food, gardens, wilderness and the Anthropocene.

Amanda Fortini has written for *The New York Times, The New Yorker, Rolling Stone, the New Republic, New York Magazine, The Los Angeles Review of Books, Wired, Slate* and *Salon*, among other publications. She is a contributing editor at *Elle Magazine*, and has been the William Kittredge Visiting Professor at the University of Montana. Her essays have been widely anthologized, including in *Best American Political Writing* and *Best of Slate*, and she was nominated for a James Beard Foundation Journalism Award.

Tami Haaland is the author of two books of poetry: *When We Wake in the Night*, and *Breath in Every Room*, winner of the Nicholas Roerich Prize. Her poems have appeared in many magazines and anthologies and have been featured on *The Writer's Almanac, Verse Daily*, and *American Life in Poetry*. Recently her work was included as part of a collaborative film installation in England, and her prose has appeared in *American Art Review* and *These Living Songs*, an anthology focused on Montana's historic and contemporary poets. She teaches at Montana State University Billings and was Montana's fifth Poet Laureate.

During his legendary writing life, **Jim Harrison** (1937-2016), published thirty-nine books of poetry, nonfiction, and fiction, including *Legends of the Fall, The Road Home*, and *Dalva*, with a posthumous volume of food-related essays, *A Really Big Lunch*, forthcoming from Grove Atlantic in 2017. His work is translated into twenty-seven languages, and an extensive literary archive is housed at Grand Valley State University. With a fondness for open space and anonymous thickets, he divided his time between Paradise Valley, Montana, and the mountains of southern Arizona.

Max Hjortsberg is a poet and grassroots conservationist residing in Livingston, MT with his family. He has called Montana home for most of his life, living and working with his feet in the water and his head in the clouds. He is the author of the chapbook, *Bonnie & Clyde (An American Daydream)*. His poems have appeared in the collections *Privacy Policy: The Anthology of Surveillance Poetics* and *An Elk River Books Reader*, as well as in *Talking River, Big Sky Journal, The Whitefish Review, Cirque Journal*, and *The Café Review*.

William "Gatz" Hjortsberg has published twelve books and is the author of numerous screenplays (notably *Legend*, directed by Ridley Scott). His novels include *Alp, Gray Matters*,

Nevermore, Falling Angel (translated into 19 languages and made into the film, *Angel Heart*), and his most recent, *Mañana*. He wrote the definitive biography of Richard Brautigan, *Jubilee Hitchhiker: The Life and Times of Richard Brautigan*. His work has appeared in *Playboy, Esquire, Sports Illustrated, Penthouse, Men's Journal, the Cornell Review* and other periodicals. Born in New York City, Hjortsberg has been a Montana resident for more than 40 years and lives in Livingston with his wife, landscape artist Janie Camp.

John Holt's latest novel is *Death in a Live Forest* was just published by New Pulp Press. His novels, *Where Paradise Lay,* based on the proposed Seven-Up Pete goldmine in the upper Blackfoot River drainage, and *The Lost Patrol*, were published by Absolutely Amazing eBooks in 2016. He and his wife, Ginny, fish and hang out in sparsely-populated country, mainly the remoteness found on northern high plains in Montana and connected country that runs north into the Yukon and Northwest Territories. They've completed articles for magazines including *The Flyfish Journal, Crossroads, Men's Journal* and *Big Sky Journal*.

Greg Keeler has published two memoirs, *Waltzing With the Captain: Remembering Richard Brautigan* (Limberlost) and *Trash Fish: a Life* (Counterpoint). Limberlost also published *Almost Happy*, his latest of seven collections of poetry. Three of his poems have been featured on Garrison Keillor's *Writers' Almanac*, and NPR's *Car Talk* aired his song "WD-40 Polka." He illustrated Jim Harrison's chapbook, *Livingston Suite*, and his paintings have been exhibited in galleries in Bozeman, Livingston and Butte and have appeared in such magazines as *FlyFish Journal, Big Sky Journal* and *Distinctly Montana*.

Alan Kesselheim has lived in Montana since the early 80s. His freelance career has followed his passions, not the least of which has been the Yellowstone River. His latest books are *Montana: Real Place, Real People* and *Let Them Paddle*.

Joan Kresich is a long time educator now working to bring restorative justice and sustainable practices to her community. She is the co-founder of HOOP Community Circles in Livingston MT, and Transition Town Livingston. She is the chair of Yellowstone Bend Citizens Council. Joan's poetry and prose have appeared in *Adanna Literary Journal, Chrysalis Reader, HeART Online, Albatross, CounterPunch* and *Snowy Egret*, among others. She lives in Livingston, Montana and Berkeley, California, in one place listening to the cries of wild geese, and in the other, the tumble of urban dialects.

Ken McCullough was born in Staten Island, grew up in Newfoundland, and considers the mountains of Montana and Wyoming to be his spiritual home. He returns every year to hike the backcountry. He lives now in Winona, Minnesota, where he is Winona's Poet Laureate. *Broken Gates*, his most recent book of poetry, is his eighth. McCullough has also collaborated with Cambodian poet U Sam Oeur, a Pol Pot survivor, on a bilingual edition of U's poetry, *Sacred Vows*, and a memoir, *Crossing Three Wildernesses*. McCullough is married to playwright Lynn Nankivil.

Brant Oswald is a fly fishing guide and instructor based in Livingston, Montana. He has written extensively for fly fishing periodicals—as a columnist for both *The Angler's Journal* and *Wild Trout Journal*, and as a contributor to *Big Sky Journal, Fly Fishing Retailer, Rod & Reel* and *Wild on the Fly*, as well as *Tight Loop* and *Flyfisher*, both Japanese fly fishing magazines. Brant has been active with conservation groups, including CalTrout, the Joe Brooks Chapter of Trout Unlimited and the Park County Environmental Council, and he served on the Governor's Upper Yellowstone River Task Force from 1997 to 2003.

Doug Peacock is the author of *Grizzly Years, ¡Baja!, Walking It Off: A Veteran's Chronicle of War and Wilderness*, and co-author (with Andrea Peacock) of *The Essential Grizzly: The Mingled Fates of Men and Bears*. A Vietnam veteran and former Green Beret medic, Peacock has published widely on wilderness issues. He was the model for Edward Abbey's infamous character, George Washington Hayduke, and received both Guggenheim and Lannan fellowships for his work on his latest book, *In the Shadow of the Sabertooth: Global Warming, the Origins of the First Americans and the Terrible Beasts of the Pleistocene*.

Ilona Popper is the author of the poetry book, *Break*. Her poems have appeared in journals and anthologies, including the *Beloit Poetry Journal* and the *Antietam Review*, and as performance pieces, solo and in collaboration with dance and theatre groups. Ilona has coached and taught writers for more than forty years. She writes articles and film scripts about wildlife, drawn from her life at the edge of Yellowstone National Park, and is active in the grassroots Montana environmental group, Bear Creek Council. More at ilonapopper. wordpress.com.

Bernard Quetchenbach's writings have appeared in a variety of books, journals, and anthologies. His work has recently been published, or is forthcoming, in *The Ecopoetry Anthology, Yellowstone Color It Wild*, and *Thinking Continental: Writing Local in a Global World*. He was a 2015 Absaroka-Beartooth Wilderness Foundation Artist-in-Residence and is a Fellow of the International League of Conservation Writers. He has published two books and two chapbooks of poetry, the most recent of which is *The Hermit's Place*, published by Wild Leaf Press. His essay collection *The Music of Circumstance* is forthcoming from Oregon State University Press. He teaches literature and writing at MSU Billings.

Shann Ray grew up in Montana. He spent some of the best years of his life in Paradise Valley, walking the mountains, body floating the Yellowstone, jumping off bridges into clear water. An NEA Fellow, his poetry and prose have been honored with the American Book Award, the High Plains Book Award in poetry and fiction, and the Bakeless Prize. He is the author of *Balefire: Poems, American Masculine: Stories*, the novel *American Copper* and *Forgiveness and Power in the Age of Atrocity*. He teaches leadership and forgiveness studies at Gonzaga University and has served as a visiting scholar in Asia, Africa, Europe and South America. Because of his wife and three daughters, he believes in love.

Myers Reece is a writer and editor based out of Whitefish, Montana. His journalism, essays and fiction have appeared in newspapers and magazines across the country, including *USA Today, San Francisco Chronicle, The Drake, Montana Quarterly, Whitefish Review, Big Sky Journal* and more. He was a founding member of the *Flathead Beacon*, where he was previously senior writer and now is an editor. He also writes for and edits *Flathead Living*, an award-winning quarterly magazine. He completed his first novel manuscript in the summer of 2016 and, at last observation, was waiting for the pile of pages to morph into a published book. More at myersreece.com.

Russell Rowland is a third-generation Montanan, born in Bozeman in 1957. His first novel, *In Open Spaces*, came out in 2002. His second and third novels, *The Watershed Years* and *High and Inside* were both finalists for the High Plains Book Award. His latest book is *Fifty-Six Counties: A Montana Journey*. He lives in Billings, where he teaches writing workshops and does private consultation with other writers.

Toby Thompson is the author of five books of nonfiction: *Riding the Rough String: Reflections on the American West,*

Metroliner, Saloon, The '60s Report and *Positively Main Street: Bob Dylan's Minnesota*. He has written for magazines as diverse as *Vanity Fair, Esquire, Playboy, Men's Journal, Outside, Big Sky Journal* and the *New York Times*. He teaches nonfiction in the creative writing program at Penn State, but lives part of each year in Livingston. He first visited Montana in 1959, working as a ranch hand near West Yellowstone. That summer he stepped off the train at Livingston, saw the town and its mountains, and hasn't stopped coming back.

Richard Wheeler is a retired newsman, book editor and novelist who has lived in Montana most of his adult life.

Todd Wilkinson, who lives in Bozeman, has been writing about the environment for 30 years. He is a correspondent for *National Geographic* and *The Christian Science Monitor* and his work has appeared in dozens of prominent magazines and newspapers with assignments that have taken him around the world. He also is author of several acclaimed and award-winning books, including the recent *Grizzlies of Pilgrim Creek, An Intimate Portrait of 399, the Most Famous Bear of Greater Yellowstone* and *Last Stand: Ted Turner's Quest to Save a Troubled Planet*.

Terry Tempest Williams has been called "a citizen writer," a writer who speaks out eloquently on behalf of an ethical stance toward life. A naturalist and fierce advocate for freedom of speech, she has shown us how environmental issues are social issues that ultimately become matters of justice. Her most recent book is *The Hour of Land: A Personal Topography of America's National Parks*. Past books include *Refuge, When Women Were Birds*, and *The Open Space of Democracy*. She is co-editor of the anthology *Testimony: Writers of the West Speak on Behalf of Utah Wilderness*, which was instrumental in the creation of Utah's Grand Staircase-Escalante National Monument. More at CoyoteClan.com.

Take Action

Voice your concern with Montana's elected officials, who need to hear from constituents and U.S. residents alike:

Senator Jon Tester
406-586-4450 | tester.senate.gov

Senator Steve Daines
406-587-3446 | daines.senate.gov

Congressman Ryan Zinke
406-502-1435 | zinke.house.gov

Governor Steve Bullock
406-444-3111 | governor.mt.gov

Stay up-to-date on the issues via local and national organizations working to defend Greater Yellowstone:

Park County Environmental Council
www.envirocouncil.org

Yellowstone Gateway Business Coalition
www.yellowstone-gateway.com

Greater Yellowstone Coalition
www.greateryellowstone.org

Bear Creek Council
www.northernplains.org/our-local-groups/bear-creek-council/

National Parks Conservation Association
www.npca.org

Earth Justice
www.earthjustice.org

CPSIA information can be obtained
at www.ICGtesting.com
Printed in the USA
FFOW05n1857201216

9 780986 304026